Salad Crops

Marshall Cavendish London & New York

Edited by Robin Wood

Published by Marshall Cavendish Books Limited
58 Old Compton Street
London W1V 5PA

This material has previously appeared in the Marshall Cavendish
partwork *Grow Your Own*.

First printing 1979

Printed in Great Britain
by Henry Stone and Son Limited
Banbury

ISBN 0 85685 478 6

Introduction

Freshness is the key to crisp, tasty salads. Tender young lettuce straight from the ground; ripe, red tomatoes plucked from the bush; freshly picked mushrooms . . . these and the five other favourites featured in this book can be produced in your garden for eating in perfect condition. Not only will they taste better and cost far less than any you can buy in the shop—their food value is greater too.

Each chapter deals with a single crop, and gives you the detailed and comprehensive instructions you need to grow it to perfection. We begin with the basic facts about the crop—sowing to harvesting time, size and yield—to help you to plan your garden. Three types of symbols, explained below, are used to give an at-a-glance guide to the nature of the crop.

Then we give full details, with clear step-by-step illustrations, on preparing the soil, sowing the crop, caring for it during growth, harvesting and storing, and even preparing your prize products for exhibition.

Of particular value are the separate sections on identifying and combating the pests and diseases that threaten your products, as well as the guides to the most popular varieties available for you to choose from.

Practical both in size and format, *Salad Crops* will soon have earned its place on your gardening shelf.

low yield	minimum effort	crops in three months or less
medium yield	needs more care	crops in 4–12 months
high yield	requires special attention	crops in over 12 months

Contents

Salad Crops

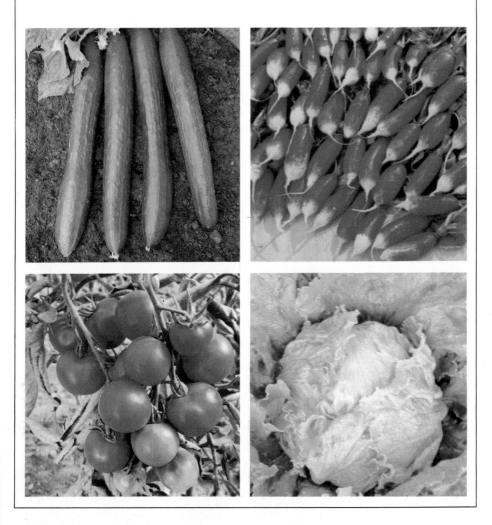

Celery

Apium graveolens
(fam. *Umbelliferae*)
Biennial, grown as an annual
Size: 30-50 cm (12-20″) high,
7.5-10 cm (3-4″) in diameter
Sowing to harvesting time: 6-8 months; mature plants of
winter celery may be left in the ground for several more
months and lifted as required
Yield: 12-15 plants, each 0.7-1 kg (1½-2 lb), per 3 m (10′) row

Celery has long been considered a specialists' crop, largely because of the labour and skill thought to be involved in trenching and blanching. In fact, these operations are not particularly difficult or time-consuming. Self-blanching and green varieties are now available if you want to grow celery with a minimum of effort.

There are three basic types of celery; winter, or blanching; summer, or self-blanching, and American green, grown for its green stalks.

Winter celery may be white, pink or red. The white varieties are rather tender and are the first to mature, followed by the pink and then the red varieties. Winter celery is available in dwarf or tall forms. If you have a small family, or do not use a lot of celery, select a dwarf variety for planting. Celery is at its best when eaten fresh; there is no point in growing giant varieties if it takes days for your family to finish one head.

The summer varieties are creamy-white, stringless, and have a milder flavour than the winter types. These are less hardy, and must be harvested before the first autumn frosts. They are not strictly speaking self-blanching, but simply contain less chlorophyll than the winter varieties.

American green celery, also for autumn harvesting, is hardy and grows happily outside, requiring no blanching. Both green and summer celery require less work than the winter varieties, and are quicker to come into crop. If you are a beginner or have little time to spend in your garden, it might be advisable to grow a summer or green variety.

Suitable site and soil

Choose a sunny open spot; celery does not do well in the shade. Like wild celery, which grows in marshes, cultivated celery needs plenty of water. The water supply must be continual as well as abundant; if celery suffers from lack of water at any time during its growing period, stunted plants or bolting will result.

SOWING CELERY

1. Sow the seeds under glass from early to mid-spring. Sow them thinly in seed compost; cover with a fine layer of compost.

2. When you can hold the seedlings between finger and thumb, prick them out 5 cm (2″) apart into boxes.

Celery needs deep, fertile, well-drained soil. It also needs soil which can retain moisture; it grows best in Fenland conditions. Sandy soils are least suitable because they tend to dry out in summer. Avoid badly-drained or heavy clay soils, which can become waterlogged. Celery is a very greedy feeder, and can be grown on well-rotted manure or garden compost without any soil added.

Raising seedlings

The sowing procedure for winter and summer celery is basically the same. Sow white winter varieties in early spring to eat in early winter. Sow pink and red sorts a month later, for harvesting in mid or late winter. Summer and green celery are usually sown in mid-spring, because earlier sowings may bolt, while later ones may be injured by frost.

If you are growing celery from seed, make sure it is guaranteed disease-free. Always wash your hands after dealing with celery seeds as they are treated with strong chemicals to prevent disease. Never use seeds intended for sowing to flavour food.

Celery seeds are slow to germinate, and may take up to six weeks under a cloche or cold frame; germination can be patchy under these conditions. Because celery has a long growing season, you should start the seeds under glass. Sow the seed thinly in John Innes seed compost and cover with a thin layer of compost. Germination will not take place unless a temperature of 15–21°C (60–70°F) is maintained; germination will be quicker if the temperature is higher.

When the first true leaf appears, prick the seedlings out into boxes, spacing them 5 cm (2″) apart. Now you can lower the temperature to 15° C (60° F). When they are growing well begin to harden them off before finally planting out. To get a longer season for celery, and avoid a sudden glut, do not plant the seedlings out all at once. Prick out and plant the most advanced seedlings first, leaving the slower ones to plant out at weekly intervals.

If you do not have a greenhouse, you can buy plants ready for transplanting.

Growing winter celery

Preparation for planting should be done well in advance, preferably in late winter. For winter celery, dig a trench 37 cm (15″) wide for a single row of plants, 45 cm (18″) for a double trench. If you are digging more than one trench, leave 1.2-1.5 m (4-5′) between trenches.

Dig out 30-60 cm (1-2′) to start with and fork over the bottom of the trench.

3

WINTER CELERY

1. Dig a trench 37-45 cm (15-18″) wide and 30-60 cm (1-2′) deep in late winter. Fork over bottom of trench to loosen soil; work in organic matter. Then cover with 7.5-10 cm (3-4″) topsoil. Make finished trench level 15-20 cm (6-10″) lower than ground. Space plants 22 cm (9″) apart.

2. If your soil is not too dry, plant quick catch crops on the ridge of soil next to the trench. Lettuce, dwarf beans, or radishes can be raised this way and harvested before the soil is needed for earthing-up in late summer.

Replace some of the soil with plenty of manure, garden compost or grass cuttings. If you cannot get farmyard manure, hops manure is a good substitute. Then cover the organic matter with 7.5-10 cm (3-4″) of soil until you have the finished trench level. The final depth of the trench varies according to soil and drainage conditions. A finished trench level of 22 cm (10″) is best for light sandy soil. On heavy clay soil the trench can be 15 cm (6″) deep.

Pile up the soil from the excavation alongside the trenches in neat ridges. If the soil is not too light, you can grow quick catch crops, such as lettuce or radishes, on them until you need the soil for earthing-up in late summer. The crops will be harvested before then.

Planting out

Two weeks before planting, apply superphosphate at the rate of 60 g per sq m (2 oz per sq yd). Right before planting, clean out of the trench bottom any soil which has crumbled in from the sides.

3. In late summer begin earthing-up. Remove side-shoots, suckers and tiny leaves; remove and destroy slugs. Wrap plants in newspaper and tie with raffia to keep soil from getting into celery heart. Place 10 cm (4″) soil from adjacent ridge around base of each plant. Earth-up gently to avoid bruising.

4. Earth-up twice more, once in late summer and again in early autumn. Each time add another 10 cm (4″) to the soil around the plants. After the final earthing-up, only the leaves should be visible. Finish the ridge off neatly with smooth sloping sides.

Then thoroughly drench the trenches with water.

Plant out the young celery in late spring, if the weather is not too cold, or early summer. Be careful not to disturb the rootballs when transplanting; it is best to use a trowel when lifting and planting them. Set the plants in either a single or double row, with a spacing of 22 cm (9″) in all directions. For the first few nights after they have been planted out, or if the weather turns frosty, cover the plants with cloches.

Care and development

The main requirement of all young celery plants is a continual supply of water. If the plant is allowed to dry out, coarse growth and tasteless hollow leafstalks will result. Organic top dressings are not usually needed. Do not apply nitrate-rich fertilizer because excess nitrogen makes the stalks cracked and frothy. Keep the trenches weed free; pick off and burn any leaves infected with celery fly. If the plants are throwing out side-shoots or suckers, remove them,

5. Harvesting can begin in mid-autumn. Scrape back the soil until you see the roots.

7. When the roots are exposed, place your fork well down into the soil to avoid damaging the stems. Lever out the plant, being careful not to damage adjacent plants.

as all growths should come from the centre of the plant.

Blanching

This is usually started in late summer, when the plants are 30-45 cm (12-15″) high. Choose a fine day, when the ground is reasonably dry. Check again for sideshoots and suckers, and remove any tiny leaves which would be buried by the process of earthing-up. Remove and destroy any slugs in the trench.

Wrap the plants in newspaper and tie with raffia. This keeps the soil from getting into the heart of the celery; once soil gets into the centre of the plant rot may set in. An alternate method of tying the stalks together is to use a long length of garden twine, twisting it round the top of each plant. Remove the twine when the final earthing-up is completed.

To begin earthing-up, rake the loose soil from the adjacent ridge down into the trench bottom. Place around the base of each plant 10 cm (4″) of soil. Do this gently, as earthing-up is done to keep out light, not to physically constrict the plant. Never apply fertilizer to the soil which is used for earthing-up, as it can damage the stalks. Earth-up around the plants twice more, in late summer and early autumn. Each time add another 10

cm (4″) to the soil around the plants, until only the top leaves are showing.

When earthing-up is finished, the trench should be filled in and formed into a ridge on the top. Finish the ridge off neatly, with smooth sloping sides. This helps throw off the rain.

Another method of blanching is to use celery collars. These are about 15 cm (6″) high and are tied round the celery. Collars are placed one on top of the other over the plant at three week intervals until celery is completely covered. Heap soil around collars to keep them from blowing in the wind.

Protection and harvesting

Once earthing-up has been completed, winter celery can remain in the ground for several months. Leave the plants in the ground for at least six to eight weeks after the last earthing-up. This will complete the blanching process, and moderate frost improves the flavour. Lift the heads from late autumn onwards, as you need them.

In very bad weather, protect the plants from frost and rain by covering the ridges with clean straw or bracken. Alternatively, place two boards on edge along the ridge; this will help throw off the rain as well. A third method of

SUMMER CELERY

Transplant young plants into frames in mid to late spring, depending on weather conditions. Space them 22 cm (9″) apart in each direction. Cover only the roots with soil; if the stems are covered, suckering will be encouraged. Water in well after planting.

protection is to place waterproofed paper along the ridge, folded down the middle in a tent shape. Fix the paper with crossed canes so it cannot be blown away by the wind.

When harvesting, work your way down one row at a time, lifting the heads in order. Carefully remove the earthed-up soil from around the plant you are lifting until you can see the roots. Then place your fork under the plant and lever it out. Be careful not to damage adjacent plants.

If a heavy or prolonged frost threatens, you can lift a few heads of winter celery in advance and store them until needed. Dig the plants out, before the ground becomes frozen solid, complete with roots. Remove any damaged stalks and outside leaves and pack them upright in a box filled with a layer of moist sand. Store the boxes in a cellar or shed, where the temperature is just above freezing point. Keep the soil moist until all the celery has been used.

After harvesting, put the leaves, outer stems and roots on the compost heap and level the ridges. The soil is already enriched for succeeding crops. Do not replant the site with carrots, which are a member of the same family, to prevent the build-up of pests and diseases.

Growing summer celery

Summer, or self-blanching, celery is not grown in trenches, but in prepared beds or cold frames. They are basically less hardy than winter celery, and mature earlier in the season. Bring on your seedlings as already described, or buy young plants.

Although it is called 'self-blanching', summer celery will be whiter if it is shaded from sunlight. You can either grow it in the open or in a cold frame. If you are growing it in the open, plant the celery in large, square blocks, say seven rows of seven, so that the outer plants cast shade on the inner ones and blanch them. As this method only works with large quantities of celery, the average household would do better to grow a smaller crop in a cold frame.

To grow summer celery in the open, prepare the soil as in late winter, digging in manure or compost at the rate of one bucketful load per sq m (sq yd). Do not dig a trench; the plants are grown on flat beds, spaced 22 cm (9″) apart in each direction. Erect a framework around the plants, and cover it with sacking, hardboard, or black plastic sheeting to keep the outside plants blanched. As with winter celery, keep the weeds down and never let the soil dry out.

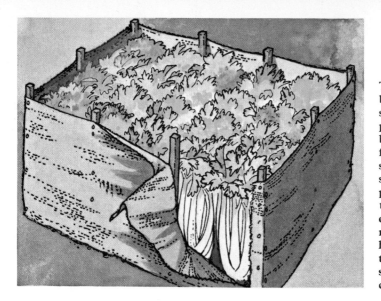

To improve the blanch of summer celery, plant it in square blocks. Erect a framework of stakes and sacking or plastic around the plants to exclude light. As rows are harvested move the frame in, to shade remaining celery.

It is easier to blanch summer celery in a cold frame, because the frame sides keep out the light. Prepare the soil well in advance, mixing in manure or garden compost. The soil mixture must be moisture-retentive, so add plenty of peat. Set the plants out in mid to late spring, depending on sowing time and weather conditions. Plant them in rows 22 cm (9″) apart covering only the roots with soil. Carefully firm the soil round the roots. Do not bury the stalks, as suckering will be encouraged. Immediately after planting water them thoroughly. Keep the frame light on for the first couple of days after planting. For a further week or so, leave the frame light open during the day, shutting it at night to keep out frost. When all danger of frost has passed, leave the frame light off.

To make full use of the cold frame, interplant the young celery with lettuces sown in mid-spring. The lettuce should be ready for harvesting in mid-summer, before the celery is ready for blanching.

Keep the frames well weeded, inspect frequently for slugs, and make sure the soil never dries out. In mid-summer, after the lettuce is lifted, dress the celery twice at ten-day intervals with a mixture of one part old soot to three parts lime.

Dust the plants with this mixture early in the morning and wash if off the next morning with a hose or watering can with a fine rose. Alternatively you can improve the blanch of summer celery, whether open grown or in a cold frame, by packing clean dry straw in between the plants to a depth of 22 cm (9″). Dust the straw with pyrethrum powder to keep the woodlice away. Loosen the straw with a fork after heavy rains, so that it does not compact around the stalks and damage them.

American Green celery
This celery is eaten green. As it is hardy and is not meant to be blanched, it is best grown in the open ground rather than a cold frame. Cultivate as for summer celery, setting the young plants outdoors in early summer, 22 cm (9″) apart and 30 cm (12″) between rows. Give cloche protection to young plants. If there is the threat of frost, give protection to all growing plants.

Harvesting and aftercare
Summer and American Green celery are harvested from late summer to mid-autumn. They should be cleared before the first autumn frosts. If the summer celery is open-grown, remember to

move the framework as you lift the plants, to keep the remaining plants blanched. Fill holes left by individual plants with clean dry straw, to prevent sunlight reaching the other celery.

Exhibition tips

Timing is a main consideration when planning to show celery at summer exhibitions, because only winter celery will grow to the standard required, and it is not normally ready until mid-autumn. For a late summer show, you must sow the seeds in mid-winter in a well-heated greenhouse. Prick out the seedlings into 12 cm (5″) deep containers, and continue growing them under glass until they can be hardened off outdoors in frames. Plant out in late spring, with cloche protection for the first fortnight. Then follow blanching and cultivation for ordinary growing.

To select celery for showing, unwrap and throw away all coverings. Tie string gently around the tops of the plants so that the stalks do not fall away. Dig them up, chopping away most of the root.

After carefully lifting the celery you wish to exhibit, wrap it in clean damp paper with roots standing in water. Do not expose the celery to light, or it will turn green.

Right before the show, lay the celery out on a table, removing the temporary tie from the top. Also remove any damaged or unwanted stalks and leaves. Trim the roots back to the hard base, leaving a pointed shaped piece at the butt. Then hold it upside down and wash with a strong spray of water from a tap or hose until it is free of all soil. Never scrub celery. Tie around the celery where the foliage joins the stalks and wrap again.

A single dish should contain three heads of celery, exhibited so the heads lie flat on the bench. If the celery is entered as part of a collection of vegetables, then six heads of celery are shown.

The judges will look for large solid heads without any coarseness or flower stems. The leaf stalks should be thick, well-balanced, clean and brittle.

Pests & Diseases

Celery fly: this is the most serious pest likely to attack celery. The insect reproduces twice, and sometimes three times a year: a first brood appears in mid or late spring, again in mid and late summer, and some years a third time in early and mid-autumn. The flies, which are 5 mm ($\frac{1}{5}$″) long, lay eggs on the leaves; the emerging maggots tunnel through the leaves causing blisters. Eventually the whole leaf shrivels and dies. If a plant loses too many leaves, it cannot grow properly and the sticks will be stunted and bitter.

Before planting out, check all plants carefully for blistered leaves; remove and burn any you find. Never leave them on the ground or put them on the compost heap. To deter the flies from laying eggs on the leaves, dust very lightly once a week with a mixture of three parts soot to one part lime. Alternative methods are to spray occasionally with derris or hang paraffin-soaked cloth near the celery. If the leaves are attacked, spray with malathion, as advised by the manufacturers, to kill the maggots, or crush them in their burrows between finger and thumb.

Celery beetle: these metallic blue oval beetles are 3 mm (1″) long and attack celery crops in mid and late summer. Swarms of them may settle on the plants; they eat the leaves first and then the hearts. Apply derris dust as soon as the beetles are seen.

Carrot fly larvae: these small yellowish maggots will occasionally attack celery roots, causing the plants to wilt and die. They are particularly active on light soils and in dry weather. In early summer the adult flies lay eggs on the soil near the plants; the emerging legless, colourless grubs tunnel through the soil into the roots. A second generation of carrot flies occasionally appears in late summer. As a preventive measure, treat seeds with a dressing containing g-HCH (BHC), or water a trichlorphon solution into the soil near the plants. Mulch the beds with grass mowings, as this tends to repel the flies.

Slugs: these common garden pests may feed on the leaf stalks if the celery is not properly earthed-up. Eventually, considerable damage may be done to the heart, and the celery may be ruined for eating or exhibition. They feed at night, leaving silvery slime trails behind them; during the day they hide in dark plant debris, under pots or boxes.

Apply metaldehyde spray to the soil and plants or bran mixed with Meta fuel, repeating if necessary. An alternative method is a 10 cm (4″) wide strip of Jeye peat around the base of the plant. Proprietary slug baits are more effective; the most effective method is to strip away all cover once a week, remove and destroy any slugs, and apply metaldehyde to the soil before replacing the cover.

Celery leaf spot: this is the most serious fungal disease. It is prevalent in wet summers and can spread rapidly by means of spores. It is seen on the leaves and sometimes the stalks as small brown spots with little black fruiting bodies developing eventually. The disease is seed-born; the best precaution is to buy seed advertized as 'thiram-treated' or 'hot-water-treated'. But remember that these treatments are only a precaution, not necessarily a guarantee that the disease will not occur.

If an attack develops, spray seedlings and young plants with benomyl, Bordeaux mixture or a fungicidal compound containing copper. Remove and destroy all infected leaves as soon as you see them. Give the plants an extra application of potash-high fertilizer to avoid soft growth, which is particularly susceptible. Where the attack is very bad, disinfect the frames with a 2% formalin solution.

Celery heart rot: this is due to a bacteria which can turn the centre of the plant into a soft, brown, slimy mess which frequently extends up the stalks. The bacteria can only enter the plant through wounds, such as those caused by slugs, careless cultivation, or frost. Keep the plants carefully earthed-up, doing so when the soil is friable and dry. Apply copper lime dust at the same time as a precaution. In severe weather protect the foliage, as the rot sometimes enters from the top of the plant and works its way down. Another precaution is to change the site for planting celery every four or five years, as the bacteria builds up in the soil. Make sure slugs are controlled, as they are often a cause of the primary wound that allows the bacteria to enter.

Boron deficiency: if your celery is stunted, with yellowing, withered leaves and dark cracks in the stalks, it is probably suffering from boron de-

Murphy Chemicals Ltd

Damage to the leaves of celery caused by the leaf-mining caterpillar of the celery fly.

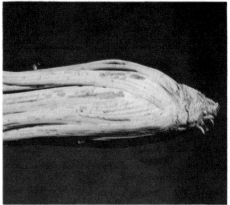

Royal Horticultural Society

Damage caused by slugs feeding on the stalks of celery. Control with slug baits or traps.

GUIDE TO CELERY TROUBLES

Symptom	Probable cause
Leaves develop blisters, then shrivel and die	Celery fly
Leaves and stalks eaten	Celery beetle
Roots eaten, plants wilt and die	Carrot fly larvae
Leaf stalks eaten, silvery slime around plants	Slugs
Small brown spots with black fruiting bodies on leaves	Celery leaf spot
Cen're of plants brown, slimy, rotten	Celery heart rot
Celery stunted, yellow withered leaves, dark cracks in stalks	Boron deficiency
Young plants, seedlings die; roots discoloured reddish brown	Damping off
Plants stunted, leaves mottled, distorted	Arabis mosaic virus
Celery bolts, stalks split and frothy	Nitrogen excess

ficiency. To correct, step up feeding with organic mater; seaweed is particularly good.

Damping off: young plants and seedlings will wilt and die when infected with damping off fungus. The roots are usually discoloured reddish-brown. Overcrowded seedlings, or those growing in too wet soil or very high temperatures are particularly susceptible. Seeds prepared with a thiram or captan dressing are less susceptible. If seedlings are attacked, spray with a Cheshunt compound, captan or zineb.

Virus diseases: there are several virus diseases which affect celery, including cucumber mosaic virus and arabis mosaic virus. Yellowing, mottling or chlorosis of the leaves and stunting of the plants are symptoms of virus infections. Cucumber mosaic virus can be transmitted from cucumbers, spinach and marrows, so do not plant celery too close to them. Arabis mosaic virus is transmitted by eelworm, so avoid planting in eelworm-infested soil.

Nitrogen excess: if there is an excess of nitrogen in the soil the celery will bolt and stalks split. Correct this by applying 45 g (1½ oz) of superphosphate and 15 g (½ oz) sulphate of potash per sq m (sq yd) or give less organic matter.

Varieties

Winter

Giant Pink—Unrivalled Pink: pale pink colour, excellent flavour; solid sticks of extreme length, good for exhibition and for the table.

Giant Red: reliable keeping quality, solid stem of dark red colour, robust grower.

Superb Pink: good for exhibition work, blanches easily and quickly, crispy texture.

Giant White-Solid White: large solid, good for table use from mid-autumn to mid-winter, recommended for exhibition work.

Prizetaker White: excellent for table and exhibition; solid, crisp stems.

Summer

Golden Self-Blanching: dwarf variety, very early cropper, ready for use in late summer; tender stringless heart and stems.

Green

American Green (Green snap): pale green stems, crisp excellent flavour; starts cropping in mid-autumn; blanching is not necessary.

Chicory

Cichorium intybus (fam. *Compositae*)
Perennial, grown as an **annual**
Sowing to harvesting time: 26-29 weeks from sowing to lifting the roots, which are then stored and forced at intervals during winter and spring.
Size: leaves grow to a height of 25-30 cm (10-12″) in the first year, when harvested green; chicons (blanched shoots) 12.5-23 cm (5-9″) long.
Yield: 12-15 plants per 3 m (10′) row; each yielding 125 g (4 oz).

A fresh, crispy vegetable harvested in winter and early spring, chicory is becoming increasingly popular as an unusual, easy-to-grow, and delicious crop. Its blanched creamy white, tightly packed shoots, called 'chicons', are a real delicacy, and are available to the home grower for very little outlay in time or money. Occasionally, you can buy this vegetable from luxury food shops, but only at prohibitive prices. However, if you grow chicory, for the cost of a packet of seeds you can have heavy crops of fat chicons over a period of several months, at a time of the year when fresh vegetables are especially appreciated.

Although it is most widely known for its blanched chicons, chicory is harvested in a variety of ways, from summer onwards. At first, its unblanched green leaves, which resemble those of a dandelion, are picked and either used fresh in salads or cooked and eaten like spinach. In autumn the roots are lifted and stored for forcing chicons through the winter. Lastly, the roots of some varieties can be cut up, roasted, and ground for use as a coffee substitute, or blended with coffee to give a pleasantly bitter taste to the drink. In these days, with coffee so expensive, growing crops of chicory root for this purpose can be a real money-saver. Usually varieties which are grown for their roots have less tasty leaves than those grown for chicons, but there is one variety, *Belgian Witloof*, which can be used both as a vegetable and as a coffee substitute.

Sugar Loaf chicory is a third, and quite distinct, variety. In autumn it produces a very close head of inwardly curled leaves, a bit like a Chinese cabbage or pale cos lettuce in appearance. Because it can stand a moderate degree of frost, it is a valuable asset to the winter vegetable garden. It makes a very pleasant salad at a time when lettuce has to either be grown in artificially heated conditions or bought from the shops at top winter prices.

The chicory plant is a hardy perennial, and its bright blue, daisy-like flowers can often be seen in the countryside, particularly on chalky soils. Do not, however, dig up wild chicory and attempt to blanch it or use the roots for essence of chicory; it is a poor substitute for a named variety, and is bound to give disappointing results.

Many people are put off by the fact that blanching is necessary before chicons can be produced. This is not at all difficult, and can be done in very little space. A bit of room in an airing cupboard, attic or warm cellar is all you need. Alternatively, under the greenhouse staging is another out-of-the-way place which can be put to good use. Once the roots have been prepared and packed into boxes or pots (both very simple operations) there is nothing left to do but harvest the chicons a few weeks later.

Suitable site and soil

An open site with not too much shade is ideal; make sure it is well away from overhanging trees. The best soil for growing chicory is a light but reasonably fertile one, which is at least 60 cm (2′) deep. Avoid badly drained soils, and shallow or stony ones, which cause the roots to fork. During the autumn before sowing the following spring, double dig the soil, working in plenty of well-rotted manure or garden compost, so that it is completely absorbed during winter. Soil which has been manured for a previous crop will only need light forking over before planting.

Chicory is found growing wild on chalky soils, and prefers an alkaline soil. If your soil is acid, work in carbonate of lime (chalk) a week or two before sowing; the rate will depend on the pH of your soil.

Sowing

Dormant chicory roots are not widely available commercially, so you will probably have to raise plants from seed. This is not at all difficult, if you wait until the end of late spring before sowing. Seeds sown earlier than this will form very big roots by the time they are lifted the following autumn or winter. These large roots are more liable to bolt,

1. In the autumn before sowing, double-dig the soil; work in plenty of well-rotted manure or compost.

2. At the end of late spring, sow seeds thinly, in drills 1.5 cm ($\frac{1}{2}$″) deep, and 30-38 cm (12-18″) apart.

3. As soon as the seedlings are large enough to handle, thin them to 23-25 cm (9-10″) apart.

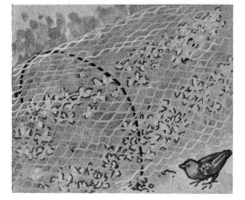

1. Birds find seedlings of *Sugar Loaf* **chicory attractive; protect seed rows with netting if necessary.**

2. Chicory is deep-rooted, so water the growing plants only if there is a severe drought.

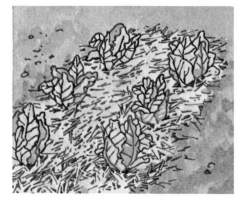

3. Mulch with clean dry straw in mid-summer to keep weeds down and also conserve soil moisture.

4. Occasionally, plants will attempt to flower; if this happens, cut out flowering stems at ground level.

Chicory flower

or go to seed, without producing chicons. If they do not bolt, they tend to form several small chicons instead of single, large, tight ones.

Before sowing, rake the soil surface to a fine tilth. Make the drills 1.5 cm ($\frac{1}{2}''$) deep, and 30-38 cm (12-15″) apart. If the soil is dry, flood the drills a couple of times with plenty of water. Sow the seeds thinly and firm the soil over the drills 25 cm (9–10″) apart. Varieties such as *Sugar Loaf* should be started in early or mid-summer, so they will be ready when few lettuces are around.

PREPARATION FOR FORCING

1. Lift the roots from early autumn onwards; only keep those with a crown diameter of 2.5-5 cm (1-2″).

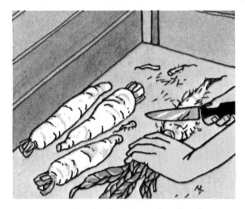

2. For storing in boxes. trim back foliage to within 2.5 cm (1″) of crown and remove all side roots.

3. Pack roots horizontally in boxes containing moist sand, and store in a frost-free shed or cellar.

Cultivation

Little cultivation is needed: water in severe droughts and hoe if weeds become a problem.

Alternatively, mulch with clean, dry straw in mid-summer, to keep weeds down.

You may find the occasional plant attempting to flower. If this happens, cut out the flowering stems at ground level.

The *Sugar Loaf* variety is sometimes troubled, in the seedling stages, by attack from birds, and some netting may be necessary. Once the plants get going, the birds find them less attractive, and they are usually left alone.

Unblanched salading

A bonus crop may be taken from some varieties by cooking the leaves like spinach, or using them fresh as green salading. During the summer, either take a few leaves from a number of plants, in order not to weaken any one of them, or reserve certain plants for this purpose.

Sugar Loaf chicory will form tightly packed white hearts in autumn, and may be cut for salad as required. Cut off the heart with a sharp knife. Alternatively, pull up the plant and trim it afterwards. The roots can be put on the compost heap, as this variety does not blanch at all well.

Preparation for forcing

Chicory roots are normally lifted in autumn and either stored in boxes indoors, or heeled in the ground until they are needed for forcing. Forcing can begin in early autumn for chicons before Christmas, and can continue through late winter—*Normato* is the best variety for early forcing. Some people leave the roots in the soil, undisturbed, until needed, but in mild weather the roots may begin sprouting prematurely.

When lifting, remember that the quality of the chicons produced is directly related to the quality of the roots. Select only strong-growing, healthy roots and consign the rest to the

15

These healthy, strong-growing roots have been lifted for forcing. Roots with a crown diameter of less than 2.5 cm (1″) tend to produce poor chicons. Those with a crown diameter larger than 5 cm (2″), on the other hand, produce several small chicons instead of one large one.

compost heap. Roots with a crown diameter of 2.5-5 cm (1-2″) are best. Any roots you leave in the soil will complete their perennial life cycle and produce flowering stems the following spring. This is only useful if you plan to save seed; otherwise, clear the site completely of all chicory roots so it can be used for another crop.

If you are heeling in the roots, lift them from early to late autumn. Pack them tightly into a deep trench, and cover the plants with enough soil or clean straw to keep the frost off. You need not trim the roots or foliage at this

stage, and heeling in should be a fairly quick operation. Dig up a few roots at a time, as you need them, from mid-autumn through early spring. Cut off the foliage to within 2.5 cm (1″) of the crown. Leave them in a frost proof shed for a week or so, to allow them to dry out. Then trim the root back to 20 cm (8″) and cut off all side roots with a sharp knife, to prepare them finally for forcing.

If you have nowhere in your garden to heel the plants in, store them in boxes. Lift and select the roots as for heeling in; late autumn is the best time to do this. Prepare them completely by trimming

1. A month before the chicons are needed, fill pots with damp sand, moist peat, potting compost or soil.

2. Put the prepared roots in vertically, 5-7.5 cm (2-3″) apart so that crowns are 2.5 cm (1″) below soil surface.

3. Invert another pot over the roots to keep the light out; remember to plug the drainage hole with a cork.

4. Begin inspecting pots a month later; the chicons are ready for harvesting when 12.5 cm (5″) tall.

5. Pull up the root and cut off the chicon afterwards; cut as close to the crown as possible.

back the foliage and removing all sideshoots. Pack the roots horizontally in boxes containing moist sand; the moisture prevents them drying out. They can be packed quite close together. Store the boxes in a cool, dry place. Temperature is most important during storage, because if it is too warm the roots may start producing shoots. On the other hand, if it is frosty the roots may be killed; ideally, the temperature should be a couple of degrees above freezing.

Forcing

About a month before the first chicons are required for the table, take out as

1. Chicons can be forced in boxes under greenhouse staging; keep out light with black polythene sheeting.

2. You can expose the crown and cut the chicon off in situ; the root will then produce a second, smaller crop.

many roots as you need; each root normally produces one chicon. For a continuous supply, lift a few roots every week or fortnight. Lifting all your roots at once will lead to a glut of chicory.

Any container which is reasonably light proof will do, provided it is deep enough to take the roots comfortably. You can use barrels, large flowerpots, black plastic bags or wooden boxes. Fill them part way up with damp sand, moist peat, potting compost or light soil. Then put the roots in vertically, 5-7.5 cm (2-3″) apart, and fill up the container with the remaining compost until the crowns are about 2.5 cm (1″) below the surface.

The problem of excluding light can be solved in three ways. The containers can be placed in an absolutely dark room or shed, in which case they will not need covering. Alternatively, cover the containers with boxes, black plastic, sacking, or inverted pots to keep the light out, remembering to allow sufficient headroom for the developing chicons. Lastly, you can cover the crowns with about 17.5 cm (7″) of additional peat, sand, or compost. Although it is a more tedious method, chicons which are forced through soil or other material tend to have more tightly packed heads than those growing without covering.

You can also force chicons in the soil

under the greenhouse staging. Use a dibber to make holes 5 cm (2″) apart. Fill the holes with water, and when it has drained away, put the roots in. Exclude light either by draping black plastic from the staging to the floor of the greenhouse, or by earthing up. Use 23 cm (9″) boards along the edge of the border to form a temporary retaining wall. Cover the planted roots with 17.5 cm (7″) of suitable material; sprinkle with water.

The roots need a minimum temperature of 10°C (50°F) to start producing shoots. If the surface of the sand or compost looks bone dry any time during forcing, sprinkle with warm water.

Depending on the heat, chicons should be ready for cutting from a month to six weeks after the roots have been planted. Begin inspecting the containers or greenhouse border after a month. Chicons are best when about 15-20 cm (6-8″) long; those forced without earthing up will be about 12.5 cm (5″) above the soil. The spear-like tops of those being forced under sand or compost will be slightly below the surface; a small mound of disturbed soil will appear directly above them. This mound indicates that the chicons are ready.

To harvest, pull up the root and cut off the chicon afterwards.

A second, smaller crop of chicons may

sometimes be taken by replacing the roots in the same container after cutting, but you will get far better results if you use fresh roots.

Exhibition tips

Blanched chicory is not often seen at major shows because there are few taking place when chicory is at its best, in winter and early spring. However, well grown chicory is worth a relatively large number of points and, should you have occasion to show blanched chicory, it is worth having a go. Twelve is the usual number of chicons required for collections, and nine for single dishes. They look best when shown upright on a small, spiked board. The board surface can be easily concealed with sprigs of fresh parsley after the chicons have been fixed into position. Remember, though, it is the chicory and not the parsley which is being shown, so use sparingly.

There are no special cultivation requirements for growing exhibition chicory. Proper packing and presentation is all-important though and, if badly presented, valuable show points can be lost. As close to the show time as possible, cut the heads with a sharp knife. Make sure there is a tiny bit of root attached, so the leaves hold together. Wipe away any soil or sand adhering to the outer leaves with a damp cloth. Roll the heads up, individually, in tissue paper, and lay them side by side in a shallow box. Exposure to light will cause the leaves to lose their blanch and turn green, so keep them covered until the last possible moment. Once they are on the staging, cover the chicons with brown paper until the judges appear.

Points will be awarded for long, solid, crisp chicons, which are well blanched and uniform in size and shape.

Unblanched chicory can be shown as part of a collection of 'salading', which is made up of three or four vegetables normally served cold. The chicory should be fresh, crisp, and perfectly clean, and displayed with the other vegetables in a shallow bowl or plate.

Pests and Diseases

Slugs: Chicory is singularly free from pests and diseases, and slugs are the only problem you are likely to encounter. These will attack chicory both above and below ground, feeding chiefly after dark. During the day they hide away in leaf litter, piles of debris, or anywhere where it is dark and moist. They are particularly prevalent on heavy, sour soils, or alkaline soils which are rich in humus and moisture.

The main signs of slug infestation are irregular holes in the leaves and roots, and faint, silvery slime trails nearby. Any poison put out for slugs must be repeated on several consecutive nights to be fully successful. Use baits based on methiocarb or metaldehyde, according to manufacturer's instructions.

Alternatively, trap the slugs in bits of decaying vegetable matter or wet sacks placed along the rows of chicory. Inspect the trails daily and remove and destroy all captured slugs.

Irregular holes in leaves and faint silvery slime trails are symptoms of slug infestation.

Varieties

Occasionally, named varieties of roots are available commercially, prepared for forcing, but it is more likely you will have to start your chicory from seed. Check with your local nurseryman.

Brussels Witloof: very popular and widely available; leaves can be blanched for spring salads, or eaten like spinach in summer; roots can be ground for coffee substitute.

Red Verona: variety with reddish tinge to foliage; when blanched, produces compact red head.

Sugar Loaf (Pain de Sucre): similar to a well grown cos lettuce in appearance; very useful for winter salads; will stand for long periods without going to seed.

Madgeburg: grown primarily for its root, which is dried, roasted and ground and used as a coffee substitute; blanched leaves and young shoots can also be used as vegetables.

Normato: new Dutch variety which is self-folding; excellent for early forcing, up to Christmas.

Red Verona

Brussels Witloof can be harvested in three ways. Although primarily used for forced chicons, the unblanched leaves produced in summer are good for salads, and the roots when roasted and ground can be added to coffee, or used as a coffee substitute.

Sugar Loaf

Normato

20

Cucumbers

Cucumus sativus (fam. *Curcubitaceae*)
Half-hardy annual
Sowing to harvesting time: 10–14 weeks
Size: plants to 2.4 m (8´) tall in the greenhouse, and 1.2 m (4´) in a frame or the open.
Yield: greenhouse cucumbers average 20 fruits per plant, ridge cucumbers 12-15.

Like many other salad crops, cucumber really is at its best fresh from the garden. With a little care it is not a difficult crop to grow well, either in the greenhouse or outdoors, and the relatively high yields per plant make it well worth the effort; just three plants will produce sufficient for the average family's needs.

Main types of cucumbers

There are two basic sorts of cucumbers. The first is the large, smooth skinned type up to 38cm (15″) long. This is often called the frame, or greenhouse, cucumber because in cool temperate climates this variety needs the protection of a frame or greenhouse. These plants are grown as climbers, so the fruits can hang down. The other main type is the ridge cucumber, so called because of the old market garden practice of growing the plants on ridges outdoors. Ridge cucumbers, which include gherkins for pickling, are shorter than the greenhouse type. They are about 13cm (5″) long, with knobbly or spiny skin.

The new, recently available Japanese varieties produce long, slim cucumbers, like the greenhouse varieties, but have the advantage of being hardy and can be grown outdoors. They are also heavy and reliable croppers.

Apple cucumbers are a novelty variety with round fruit the size of a small apple, a pale, yellowish-white skin and a good texture. They are generally regarded as more digestible then the green-fruited varieties. A trailing variety, they can be grown in pots or boxes in the greenhouse, in a frame, or outside in a warm, sheltered part of the garden.

Pollination

Cucumbers produce fruit in two ways. Wild and ridge cucumbers bear separate male and female flowers on the same plant, and the female flowers need to be pollinated before fruits are produced. Greenhouse cucumbers also bear male and female flowers, but the female flowers produce fruit without pollination. These unfertilized fruits are what you should aim to produce in the greenhouse. If your greenhouse cucumbers are fertilized the fruits swell at one end, containing hard, inedible seeds. They are spoiled for exhibition use and are bitter tasting and unpleasant to eat.

Growing under glass

You can either grow your plants from seed, or buy seedlings from a reliable source. If you buy plants, choose dark green, short, stocky ones. Select ones with three or four true leaves, and the seed leaves still intact. Do not buy chilled plants from windy shopfronts. After buying the plants, stand them in the greenhouse for a few days in their pots. This will acclimatize them to new conditions; you can then transplant them successfully into the hotbed.

Sowing

If you grow cucumbers from seed, it is best to sow them in a propagator or warm greenhouse, at an absolute minimum temperature of 15°C (60°F), but 18-25°C (65-75°F) is better. Select only plump, clean seeds and throw away any which are flat, discoloured, or very small. Sow the seeds singly in clean, 6-7.5cm (2½-3″) pots, which have been filled with John Innes seed compost to within 1.5cm (½″) of the top of the pot. Place the seeds on edge, sideways, about 1.5cm (½″) deep and lightly firm the surface. Water the compost and then cover the pots with black plastic or a sheet of glass and brown paper. Make sure the compost is thoroughly damp, because the seed casings are fairly tough. If there isn't enough moisture in the soil to penetrate the casing, the seed may not germinate. After germination, remove covering; place plants in a light position in the greenhouse. The young plants should grow rapidly and will need staking with a small, split cane. Keep the temperature at 15°C (60°F), minimum; do not let the temperature drop at night.

White roots should show on the outside of the rootball within a month of sowing; when you can see them pot the plants on into 10-12.5cm (4½-5″) pots of John Innes potting compost No. 2, or into their final positions if you can maintain a high enough temperature.

Making a hotbed

Cucumbers require a rich, moist, well drained and aerated rooting medium. Greenhouse varieties are most successfully grown in beds raised above ground level. These beds should be heated; you can use hot water pipes, ducted warm air, electric heating, or heat produced by fermenting organic matter.

RAISING GREENHOUSE CUCUMBERS

1. Sow seeds in seed compost. Gently firm the surface and water.

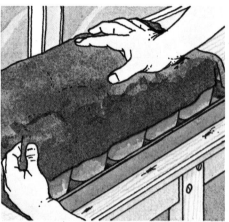

2. Cover with black plastic or brown paper and glass, until germination.

3. When white roots show on outside of rootball, pot on young plants.

4. When roots have filled 12 cm (5″) pots, nip out growing point.

5. When plants are 45 cm (18″) high, plant them into the hotbed.

6. Train the young plants up strings fixed to horizontal wires.

7. Damp down the greenhouse often, particularly in hot weather.

8. Top dress with 2.5 cm (1″) of potting compost to encourage roots.

The base of the bed can be soil, ash gravel, or concrete. Make sure the base is absolutely clean before building the bed.

If you plan to heat the bed by fermenting organic matter, put a layer of fresh manure on the base 45cm (1′6″) wide and 15cm (6″) deep. Turn this over occasionally for a few days, to allow excess nitrogen to be given off as ammonia. Another way of producing heat is to use straw. Put down a 60cm (2′) thick layer of straw, firmed down. Sprinkle it with sulphate of ammonia and saturate the straw with water. On top of the straw or manure, place a 30cm (1′) deep and 45cm (1′6″) wide layer of good soil, or John Innes potting compost No. 2, forming it into a ridge.

Planting
When the pots are full of roots, and two to four leaves have fully expanded, nip out the growing point and plant the young cucumbers into 23cm (9″) pots. When these plants have eight or nine leaves and are 37cm (1′6″) high, plant them directly in the hotbed. They should be 60cm (2′) apart, in one line down the centre of the bed.

Training
The cordon training of cucumbers is roughly similar to that of tomatoes. Fix three wires horizontally, the top one 2.1 m (7′) high, the centre wire about 1 m (3′) high and the bottom wire along the surface of the bed; all three wires should be 30cm (1′) from the outside glass of the greenhouse. Next fix a vertical string for each plant, tying it to the top, centre and base wires. Tie the leading shoot to this string at regular intervals. When the plant reaches the top wire, pinch out the growing point and tie in the lead growth. Remove all side shoots up to a height of 38cm (15″) above the base of each plant. If fruits form in the first or second leaf joints of the laterals, pinch out at two leaves beyond the fruit. If there are no fruits, stop the laterals at the second joint.

Continue tying the plant to the

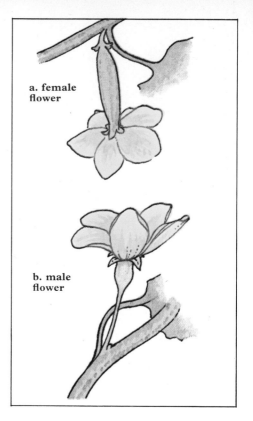

a. female flower

b. male flower

vertical string, stopping side shoots and removing all tendrils and male flowers until the top wire is reached. You can easily recognize male flowers, as they have no miniature cucumbers behind the petals. Continue removing the male flowers until the last fruits of the season are swelling. Remove any cucumbers which start to develop on the main stem.

Care and development
Cucumbers must be given plenty of moisture and warmth at all times, but particularly in hot weather. If you allow them to dry out at all, wilting plants, flabby fruits, pests and diseases will follow. The atmosphere in the greenhouse should be very humid. Damp down two or three times a day, always using water which is the same temperature as the greenhouse. Use a rotary spinkler attachment to a hose, a syringe, or a watering can with a rose spray to moisten the floors, walls, staging and

Do not remove any flowers from ridge varieties; pollination is essential to produce fruit.

pots, as well as the plants. When the temperature in the greenhouse rises above 24°C (75°F), you should provide ventilation, to keep the air circulating around the plants.

It is difficult to lay down hard and fast rules concerning feeding. It is generally considered best to apply a high nitrogen feed when the fruits start to swell; continue feeding twice weekly.

Top dress the beds with a 2.5cm (1″) layer of John Innes No. 2 potting compost once a month. This helps nourish the surface roots and also encourages new adventitious, or extra, roots to form at the base of the stem. The cucumber's thick coarse rooting system is particularly vulnerable to infection by fungus and bacteria, and may rot partway through the cropping season, so the continual production of healthy new roots is very important.

You must remember to remove the male flowers every four days, picking them off by hand. It is also a good idea to fix fine gauze to any ventilation openings in the greenhouse to exclude bees and flies which may enter and pollinate the female flowers. There are 'all female' varieties on the market; these produce very few male flowers and are capable of extremely high yields. *Femspot, Femden,* and *Femina* are some examples.

Growing cucumbers in frames
Where a greenhouse is not available, cucumbers can be grown successfully in a cold frame. The frame should have a stout wooden, concrete or brick base to retain warmth. Raise the seedlings as for greenhouse cultivation. In late spring place the young cucumber plants in the centre of the frame on a hotbed, as described earlier. If you have no hotbed, delay planting until early summer. Keep the frame closed, except for occasional ventilation on warm days, but when the weather is very warm leave the frame light off all day. Remember to replace it at night, when the temperature drops.

25

Pinch out the growing tips when four or five leaves have formed on each plant. Shortly afterwards, shoots will be produced in the axils (joints) of these leaves. Select the four strongest shoots and train one towards each corner of the frame. Carry out watering, feeding, and pinching out side shoots as described above. As the fruits develop, place a sheet of glass or piece of slate under the fruits, to keep them from becoming soiled or discoloured. Remember to remove any male flowers. Shade the plants from strong sunlight to prevent scorching.

Growing outdoors

Ridge cucumbers will grow and crop under lower temperatures and drier atmospheric conditions than the greenhouse varieties. In a mild climate you can sow the seeds directly outdoors, or under cloches in a sunny, sheltered position.

Cucumbers will grow in any well-drained soil, as long as it is not too acid. Dig in a generous helping of garden compost, well-rotted manure, or leaf mould 30cm (1′) deep and the same width. Cover this manure with the excavated soil, which is then moulded up into a low, flat-topped ridge. This allows the water to drain away from the main stem; although the roots like a lot of moisture, stem canker may set in if the base of the stems get wet. If you are having more than one ridge, leave a good 1.2m (4′) between them.

If your soil is very light, the ridge system will not work because enough moisture will not reach the roots. A good alternate method is to dig the organic matter into holes 90cm (3′) apart and 30cm (1′) deep by 60cm (2′) square. Over this place a 10cm (4″) layer of John Innes potting compost No. 3, making sure it is flush with the level of the surrounding ground. Use the soil which has been excavated from the hole to form a low mound on the north side of the plant stem. This acts as a shelter. Lightly fork in a general fertilizer at the rate of 60g per sq metre (2 oz per sq yd) two weeks

SOWING RIDGE CUCUMBERS

1. Dig compost or manure into trench and cover with soil ridge.

2. For light dry soil, dig in manure and plant cucumbers on flat.

3. Sow groups of 3 seeds 90 cm (3′) apart and 2.5 cm (1″) deep.

POT-RAISED SEEDLINGS

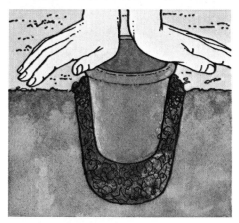

1. Before planting out, form a hole in the soil using an empty pot.

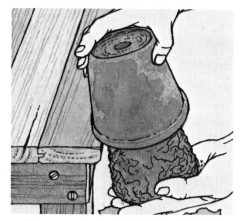

2. To remove plant from pot, up-end the pot and tap out on a table edge.

3. Put plant into preformed hole and water in with tepid water.

before planting and again when the plants are beginning to grow well.

Sow the seed in the open in late spring or early summer, as soon as the soil has warmed up, or two or three weeks earlier under cloches. Sow a group of three seeds, point downwards, on each prepared trench, 2.5cm deep (1″), or 90cm (3′) apart on the long ridges. Keep the seedlings covered with a cloche or jam jar until they are established. Then select the strongest of the three and discard the others. Never transplant seedlings sown in the open.

If you plant out seedlings sown in the greenhouse, harden the seedlings off first so they can withstand the lower temperatures.

Because cucumber roots are delicate, there is a special method of transplanting pot-grown seedlings to the open ground. First, plant an empty pot of the same size the cucumber is growing in. Firm the soil around the empty pot, and remove it with a slight twist. Now turn the cucumber plant out of its pot into the preformed cavity. Push the surrounding soil into contact with the rootball. Water it well with tepid water.

Remove the growing tips when the plants have produced six leaves. Train out the resulting side shoots, evenly spaced, stopping those which have produced fruit at the seventh leaf, and stopping further shoots if the plant needs restraining. This practice encourages the plants to devote more energy and nourishment to the swelling fruits and less to unproductive vegetative growth.

Do not remove the male flowers, as the female flowers must be fertilized before the fruits will develop. Insects usually pollinate the flowers; alternatively, you can hand pollinate the female flowers with the male flowers. Remove the male flower by its stem and carefully take off the petals. Then shake the powdery central core into the centre of the fully open female flower.

Water the plants frequently in dry weather, being very careful to keep water off the base of the main stem. Spray both

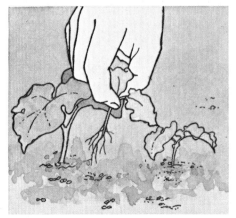

1. If directly sown, thin to one plant per group when first leaves appear.

2. Keep the plants well watered if the weather is dry.

3. Nip off the ends of side shoots one leaf beyond the young fruit.

4. To pollinate female flower brush with the anthers of a male flower.

5. Protect cucumbers from soil by placing a pane of glass under them.

6. Harvest the ridge cucumbers when they are about 12 cm (5″) long.

Greenhouse cucumbers ready for harvesting; plants should crop from early summer onwards.

sides of the foliage with tepid water on dry evenings to keep red spider mite away. Feed the plants as for greenhouse varieties, first when the fruits begin to swell, and again at fortnightly intervals. Whenever fine white roots appear on the surface, cover them with a 5cm (2″) layer of moist compost, pressed firmly down.

The outdoor Japanese varieties need supporting frames on which to grow. Buy 2.2m (7′6″) poles and insert them so they are 1.8m (6′) above the ground and 1.8m (6′) apart. Run wires between them and attach netting with a 20cm (8″)

mesh. At each end of the row, use much stouter posts, with straining wires to pegs in the ground for lateral stability. Plant the cucumbers 30cm (1') apart. Train the plants upwards, pinching out the lead growth when they reach the top of the net. Stop the side shoots as described for ridge varieties.

Harvesting

Greenhouse cucumbers will start to crop in late spring or early summer, and fruits should be cut when about 30-37cm (1'-1'3") long. Cropping should continue until autumn. Ridge cucumbers sown under cloches will begin to crop in late summer, or early autumn if they have been sown in the open ground. Outdoor cropping will continue until the first frosts, when the plants will be killed. Harvest the cucumbers when they are young and crisp; old fruits go to seed and if left on the plant cause further fruit production to cease. If you have a bumper crop, pickle them if they are the ridge variety, or give the extra cucumbers to friends or neighbours. Cucumbers are at their best when freshly picked; they do not store well.

Exhibition tips

The judges will look for straight fruits of uniform thickness, with short necks and noses. Cut the fruits early in the morning or late in the evening when they are fully charged with water. They are at their best when the two sides are approximately parallel and straight. A pointed cucumber is not yet ripe; a misshapen yellow one will not win prizes.

Cucumbers are usually shown in pairs, when between 30cm (1') and 37cm (15") long. Cut the fruit with a length of stem; it can then be handled by the stem and the bloom will not be damaged. The flower should still be on the end; the fruit should be young, crisp and tender.

If the fruits you intend to show are at their best a few days before the exhibition, cut them off the vine, and place them stem downwards in a jar of water. Change the water every day.

Pests & Diseases

The warm, moist conditions in which cucumbers flourish provide the perfect environment for bacterial and fungal infections. Since many of these are encouraged by improper watering and ventilating, make sure you are cultivating the plants properly. Be on the lookout for any sign of infection and act quickly to control it, because disease will spread rapidly in close greenhouse or frame conditions. When you use an insecticide on cucumbers, be sure to choose one that will not damage the plants; the *Curcubitaceae* family are sensitive to some chemicals sprays.

Red spider mite: this pest causes the leaves to turn yellow; if severely infected, the plant will become bronze

GUIDE TO CUCUMBER TROUBLES	
Symptoms	*Probable causes*
Leaves turn yellow; silky webs on plant	Red spider mite
Small green insects; leaves turn yellow	Greenfly
Clouds of minute insects	Whitefly
Holes in stems of young plants, silvery slime	Slugs
Holes in leaves and surface of young fruit, grey, hard shelled creatures	Woodlice
Leaves discoloured, plant collapses	Root knot eelworm
Grey fluffy growth on stems fruit and leaves	Botrytis
Leaves wilt, stem becomes dark, plant dies	Collar rot
Leaves mottled yellow; plant wilts, dies	Mosaic virus
Leaves turn yellow from base upwards	Verticillium wilt
Sunken, oozing spots on fruit	Gummosis
Wet, dark wounds on stems, leaves and fruits	Sclerotinia disease

Murphy Chemical Co.

Adult whiteflies on the underside of the leaves of cucumber foliage.

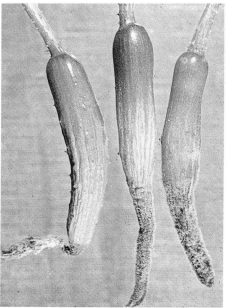

Ministry of Agriculture Fisheries and Food

Furry growths on young cucumbers produced by a severe attack of botrytis.

coloured, wilt and collapse. Another sign of red spider mite is the appearance of silky webs around the leaves and stems. The best preventative action is to maintain damp conditions in the greenhouse or outdoors. The best control is to spray the infected plants with derris or soft soap.

Greenfly: these small green insects are usually found in colonies on or near the growing points and under the leaves, which may turn yellowy green and wither. Control greenfly by smokes or sprays of malathion or nicotine. Use the nicotine with care, as overuse may blanch the leaves; if this happens, cut off the bleached leaves immediately and spray with a nicotine soap wash.

Whitefly: if, when you disturb the leaves of cucumber plants, clouds of minute insects appear, then the plants are infested with whitefly. These insects are very destructive and weakening; they feed chiefly on the sap and excrete honeydew which encourages the growth of sooty mould. Spray with malathion as soon as whiteflies are seen.

Slugs: slug damage can usually be spotted by holes in the stems of young plants and the presence of silvery slime trails. Proprietary pellets are the most effective control.

Woodlice: these are grey, minute armadillo-shaped creatures which roll up into small balls when touched. They eat holes in the leaves and may also attack the surface of young fruits. Woodlice are most likely to occur in old greenhouses or frames; spray or dust around the roots of infected plants with BHC (HCH).

Root knot eelworm: plants indoors and outdoors may be attacked by these microscopic pests which invade the roots. Leaves may become discoloured; in bad cases the whole plant may collapse. Although some plants may survive mild infections, it is best to dig up and burn any diseased plant. There is no absolutely effective control, but if one plant is infected, it is a good idea to treat the soil with a sterilant such as formaldehyde before growing susceptible crops in the same place.

Botrytis: this grey fluffy growth on the stems, fruits, and leaves is best controlled by benomyl sprays. Badly infected plants should be removed and burned, as they will never crop well.

Collar rot: this usually affects greenhouse cucumbers which are growing in

31

The roots of plants infected with collar rot are swollen, discoloured and distorted.

Leaves infected with cucumber mosaic virus display characteristic yellow mottling.

badly drained soil or have been over-watered. The plants are attacked by soil-borne organisms at or slightly above ground level. The leaves wilt, the stems become dark and the plants die. Preventive measures of raised beds, well-aerated soil, and good hygiene are useful. Plants which are not too badly damaged may be saved by removing all decaying tissue and dusting the infected areas with captan. Then raise the level of the soil 3.5cm ($1\frac{1}{2}''$) around the stem to encourage the growth of new adventitious roots. In 10 days top dress again. Pull out and destroy badly infected plants; treat the soil around adjacent plants with benomyl or captan.

Mosaic virus: the leaves of plants infected with mosaic virus become yellow and mottled; the whole plant then rapidly wilts, shrivels up and dies. As there is no effective control for the virus, and it is carried by greenfly, the best prevention is to control greenfly.

Verticillium wilt: this soil-borne fungus causes the leaves to turn yellow from the base upwards. The disease is more liable to occur in cold wet conditions. It usually attacks the roots of young plants; older plants are vulnerable if they have open wounds. Eventually the diseased plants wilt, and should be

dug up and burned. Apply Cheshunt compound to the soil before replanting.

Gummosis of cucumber: this fungus disease affects plants grown in a greenhouse or frame; it spreads quickly in cold, wet conditions. Infected fruits develop sunken spots which ooze a gummy liquid; this spot is eventually covered with dark spores. Occasionally small spots appear on the stems or leaves. Keeping the greenhouse or frame warm and well ventilated is a good preventive measure. Control gummosis by spraying with zineb or captan; destroy all diseased fruits. Disinfect the greenhouse or frame before replanting.

Sclerotinia disease: wet, dark wounds appear on the stem, leaves and fruits, followed by fluffy, white growths with black central areas. Dig up and burn any infected plants.

Anthracnose: the leaves will have small pale patches which quickly turn brown and grow bigger until the whole leaf dies; stems are sometimes affected. Remove and destroy badly infected plants. Spray the remaining plants with 1 part lime sulphur to 60 parts water with a spreading agent. Make sure that the greenhouse is well ventilated, and spray with formalin when it is empty or between crops.

Telegraph

Femspot

Varieties

Greenhouse

Telegraph Improved: reliable cropper for cold or heated greenhouses, useful for exhibition; uniform fruit of deep green colour; fine quality.

Butcher's Disease Resisting: medium-sized, slightly ribbed fruit; heavy cropper; highly resistant to leaf spot; easy to grow.

Conqueror: dark green fruits; very prolific; suitable for unheated greenhouse or frame in northern areas.

Femden: F_1 hybrid produces mainly female flowers; prolific cropper; disease resistant.

Topsy: F_1 hybrid female flowering type; sweet juicy fruits 30-40cm (12″-16″) long.

Femspot: F_1 hybrid; female flowering variety; early cropper; fruits 35cm (14″) long; disease resistant.

Femina: produces mainly female flowers; heavy yield; disease resistant.

Topnotch: F_1 hybrid; vigorous grower; enormous crops; suitable for greenhouse or frame.

Ridge varieties

Marion: Virus-resistant; fruits no tendency to bitterness; 22 cm (9″) long.

Greenline: fruits retain colour over long period; especially recommended for growing under cloches.

Burpee Hybrid: F_1 hybrid; vigorous; prolific; extra large, dark green fruit; crisp, white flesh.

Perfection: prolific cropper; fruits 12–15 cm (5–6″) crops well into autumn.

Patio-Pik: early F_1 hybrid of bushy, prolific habit; produces up to 30 fruits per plant.

Baton Vert: F. Hybrid; very early cropper; long, slender; good flavour.

Burpless Tasty Green: fruits low in acid; dark green, smooth-skinned, small white spines; 20-25cm (8-10″) long; can be sown on open ground; resistant to heat, and to powdery and downy mildew.

Nadir: F_1 hybrid; long fruited; prolific habit; outstanding variety.

Venlo Pickling: grown for gherkins for pickling; heavy consistent cropper; gather fruits when young and tender.

Japanese varieties

Kyoto: straight fruits, containing very few seeds; 5cm (2″) in diameter, 37cm (15″) long.

Chinese Long Green: smooth skinned; up to 60cm (2′) long; keeps well after harvesting.

Kaga: up to 35 cm (15″) long; early cropper; dark green with yellow stripes.

Novelty variety

Apple-Shaped: produces pale green, round fruit; prolific cropper of good flavour.

Lettuce

Lactuca sativa (fam. *Compositae*)
Half-hardy annual.
Sowing to harvesting time: 8-14 weeks
Size: Cabbage and American types between 15-38 cm
(6-15″) in diameter; cos types between 20-40 cm
(8-16″) tall.
Yield: 9-12 heads, each weighing about 224-340 g (8-12 oz),
per 3 m (10′) row.

The most popular salad vegetable, lettuce is easily grown and, with careful planning, you can have a high all-year-round yield. Tender young lettuce, freshly cut, has an unbeatable flavour and the crop is a must for every kitchen garden.

There are three main types of lettuce: cabbage varieties, which are hearted and look like cabbages, taller and crisper cos types, and the frizzy-headed loose-leaf American lettuces. Cabbage lettuces can be further divided into butterheads, with tender, butter-coloured hearts, and crispheads, which are crisper and have hearts that blanch to white. The hearts of cos lettuce are also blanched—many varieties of cos are now self-blanching with leaves which fold in by themselves. American varieties are harvested by picking single leaves, rather than by cutting the whole plant.

Lettuce has been much hybridized since the early sixties, and there are all sorts of varieties now available for growing at particular periods of the year. There are also several new dwarf lettuces available for the small garden or for container growing. Before buying your lettuce seed, study the catalogues carefully. Most catalogues specify which varieties are suitable for which season. When growing out of season, in particular, it is important to choose varieties which have been bred specially for that particular purpose, such as early spring cropping or heated greenhouse winter cropping.

Preparing the soil

Lettuces will grow well on almost any garden soil, although they prefer soil that is rich and light, well drained and dug. Clays which are well broken down produce very good plants, as will sandy or gravelly soils which have been bulked with organic matter. The site should have its humus content renewed every year with an application of farmyard manure, rich compost or green manure worked into the ground at a rate of 6 kg per sq m (13 lb per sq yd) the autumn before a spring sowing. This will also aid in water retention, which is important because lettuces are 90 per cent water and must have very moist soil to grow

1. Lettuces like an alkaline soil, so prepare the ground prior to sowing with an application of lime.

2. For early spring sowings outdoors, prepare shallow drills and sow the seed very thinly.

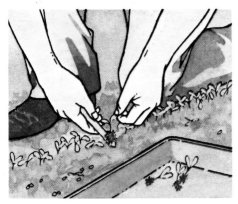

3. Thin when two leaves have formed. If thinnings are to be transplanted, handle gently by one leaf only.

4. Prepare the holes before transplanting, put the seedlings in and water the ground well.

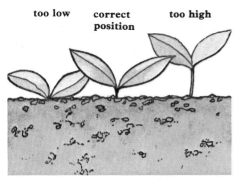

5. Take care to transplant the seedlings with the neck exactly level with the soil.

6. Seedlings can be put into the ground which has been covered with sheets of plastic to retain moisture.

	RECOMMENDED VARIETIES	GROWING CONDITIONS
SUMMER LETTUCE	Windermere	Sow outdoors at 2-week intervals for a long harvesting period.
	All the Year Round	Has one of the longest periods for cutting. Sow outdoors in spring or under cloches in autumn.
	Lobjoits Green Cos	Good summer cos type to grow outdoors.
	Salad bowl	Sow outdoors. Pick by pulling outer leaves.
AUTUMN LETTUCE	Winter Density	Good autumn cos for early cutting.
	Appia	Quick-maturing butterhead which can withstand a hot summer.
WINTER LETTUCE	Amanda	Must be forced in a heated greenhouse.
	Kordaat	Good for growing under glass with heat.
	Kwiek	For growing in a cold frame or greenhouse.
SPRING LETTUCE	Premier	Sow in frames or under cloches to protect over the winter.
	May Queen	Prefers a heated greenhouse, but can be successful under cloches in a mild winter.

KEY

sow

harvest

for greenhouse growing

for growing under cloches

Summer lettuces grown from successional sowings. The ones on the left are ready for cutting.

Bernard Alfieri

EAR-ROUND LETTUCE

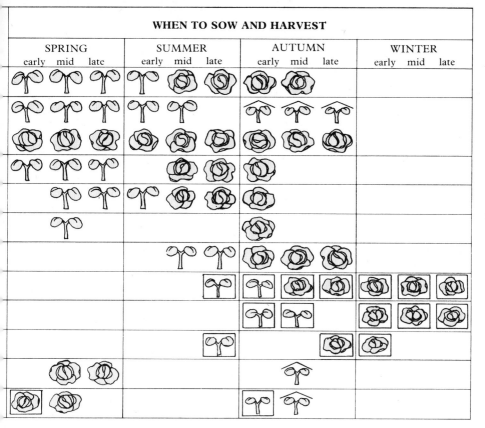

WHEN TO SOW AND HARVEST			
SPRING early mid late	SUMMER early mid late	AUTUMN early mid late	WINTER early mid late

rapidly and form well. Lettuces also need lime (a pH of 7.5 is best), so test soil and apply lime before sowing if necessary. Poor and ill-prepared soil will produce floppy leaves and failure to heart-up.

Quick-growing lettuce is a good vegetable for intercropping between rows of other vegetables, such as tall varieties of peas, providing you have prepared the soil carefully.

Planning your sowings

Lettuces can be available for harvesting throughout the year if you make successional sowings of different varieties. Classification is by the season for harvesting, not the time of sowing, so choose your varieties, whether cabbage, cos or loose-leaf types, according to your harvesting needs.

Summer lettuce: sowing outdoors can start in early spring with the first of a succession of fortnightly sowings designed to maintain a supply of lettuces from early summer until the autumn. Choose cabbage, cos or American varieties; plant a mixture to give a varied crop. Sowing several different kinds also gives varied rates of germination and development, and extends the period for cutting.

Unfortunately, a routine of successful sowings does not guarantee an uninterrupted supply of prime lettuces. Except in a steadily favourable climate, there are times when the lettuces are checked. And when the weather is hot, the whole crop engages in a race to see which plant can bolt (run to seed prematurely) first. Bolting used to be a serious problem to lettuce growers, but

To catch crop, sow lettuces between rows of peas, preferably running north to south to avoid shading.

Lettuces are ideal for growing in cold frames: sow the seed in late winter for harvesting in spring.

Extend the period of harvesting by successional sowings. Plant some lettuces every two weeks in spring.

For late winter and spring crops sow hardy varieties in autumn and protect with cloches or tunnels.

newer varieties are less likely to bolt in high temperatures, so long as they are kept well watered.

Sow the seed fairly thinly in short shallow drills about 1.5 cm ($\frac{1}{2}''$) deep and 30 cm (1') apart. The seed should germinate in about 4-12 days, and you should thin as soon as the first pair of true leaves have formed. Aim for a spacing of one plant every 23-30 cm (9-12") depending on the size of the variety.

It is best to sow lettuces where they are to remain, as transplanting can cause a check in growth. In any case, transplanting is only satisfactory very early in the growing season, as later transplants are liable to bolt. When transplanting

lettuces, lever the plants gently out of the ground with a spatula and handle only the leaves with your finger and thumb. Lower the transplants into prepared holes, then firm them down and water them well to ensure that the rootlets make good contact with the soil. Do not plant too high or the lettuces will not heart; too low planting can cause grey mould infections of the lower leaves. The neck of the plant must be exactly at soil level.

You can give transplanted lettuces a better start by putting them in a row covered by a strip of black plastic. Secure the edges of the plastic by weighting down with stones, then make

Butterhead lettuces grown under cloches and ready for cutting. These soft, round cabbage types usually grow very quickly.

cross-shaped cuts about 30 cm (12″) apart, and transplant the lettuces in the usual way. The plastic will help retain moisture in the soil.

Autumn lettuce: choose cabbage or cos types for autumn lettuce. Sow the seed as you would for summer lettuce, in succession from mid-summer to late summer. Sow where the plants are to mature. Thin the 5-7.5 cm (2-3″) high seedlings so that you have about 23-30 cm (9-12″) between plants. Your first sowings should be ready for cutting by early autumn; the last by late autumn to early winter. However, the latest sowings may be slow to grow and may not be ready by early winter. If you protect these plants with cloches or tunnels they should withstand the winter and will certainly be ready for cutting by early spring.

Winter lettuce: if you have a heated greenhouse, you can enjoy fresh lettuces from early winter through to early spring. A well-constructed and well-designed greenhouse where you can maintain a temperature of 15 C (60 F) is a necessity. However, you should keep in mind the amount of fuel needed to maintain this temperature, and consider that in a cold winter it could prove very expensive to grow your own lettuces.

If you decide to grow winter lettuce, make successive sowings in early to mid-autumn of a cabbage variety. Sow in seed trays filled with good quality compost.

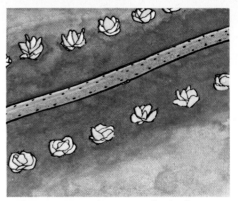

7. Weed between the young plants with a draw hoe. In addition to keeping down the weeds, this will help to discourage egg-laying insects.

8. Lettuces need a great deal of water to grow well. Keep the soil very moist; a trickle hose is ideal because water seeps out slowly.

9. Mulch the young lettuces by applying well-rotted garden compost with a fork. This will keep down the weeds and retain moisture.

10. Slugs love sweet, tender young lettuce plants. Discourage these pests by scattering slug pellets on the ground between the rows.

11. To test for firmness, apply gentle pressure to the heart with the back of your hand.

12. To harvest cabbage or cos lettuces, use a sharp knife to cut just below the lowest leaves.

Germination must take place at temperatures between 10-15°C (50-60°F). Prick out the 5 cm (2") high seedlings into boxes and plant them in cropping position, 23-30 cm (9-12") apart, as soon as the first pair of true leaves is fully developed. The greenhouse temperature should be kept at 15°C (60°F) for three weeks after planting, and thereafter maintained at 10-13°C (50-55°F). Maintaining humidity in the greenhouse (through controlled watering and ventilation) is also important, as the lettuces need a moist environment.

Spring lettuce: spring lettuce can be grown outdoors or under protection. Sowing outdoors is satisfactory only in areas where the winters are fairly mild, and even then you must choose hardy types. The crop will not survive on cold, heavy ground, so choose an open, sunny site with land well manured for a previous crop. Sow the seed in a seedbed in late summer, and plant out between mid and late autumn in rows 30 cm (1') apart, allowing 23 cm (9") between plants. Hoe the rows just before winter sets in; then leave them alone until growth restarts in early spring, when they will need the same care as spring-planted types.

Spring lettuces are generally more successful if they are protected over the winter. Follow the basic instructions above, but protect the rows with barn cloches. Thin seedlings to about 23 cm (9") apart in early winter. When growth begins again in early spring, remove the cloches a few at a time. Cutting for the plants uncloched first should begin in mid-spring.

Care and cultivation

All lettuces require warmth, moisture and a weed-free environment with protection from garden pests. The soil must be well prepared so that it is rich enough in humus to retain moisture adequately. Give the lettuces as much water as the roots require, but do not try to hurry growth by overwatering. It may

13. If you are growing a variety of cos which is not self-blanching, blanch by tying around the middle and then around the top a week later.

14. Loose-leaf lettuces are picked by pulling the outer leaves. Pull them off gently and take them straight into the kitchen.

15. To store, pull up the whole plant and tie a plastic bag around the roots. Keep in refrigerator.

be difficult in hot weather to keep soil moist and prevent a crust from forming; overcome this by mulching with well rotted organic matter. Strips of black plastic placed on the ground close to the plants will also help to retain moisture, especially if placed down just after rain.

Hoe frequently between the rows and the plants. This will kill the weeds before their roots are big enough to compete with the crop.

If you are growing one of the varieties of cos lettuce which is not self-blanching you may want to blanch the plants to increase their crispness. About two weeks before the lettuce is ready for harvesting, apply a tie of raffia or a rubber band around the thickest part of the plant. One week later, make another tie about 15 cm (6") further up. The harvested lettuces will be firm and crisp.

Cutting your lettuces

Harvest lettuces as soon as they are at their best and fully hearted. When the heart begins to form a point and push upwards, the plant is beginning to bolt and the quality will fall off rapidly. The lettuces should feel firm, so test for firmness by pressing with the back of your hand, not with your fingers which will bruise the plants.

Cut lettuces with a sharp knife, just above the lowest leaves, or pull out by the roots and cut them off. If the lettuces are going to be stored, it is best to pull the whole plant, enclose the roots in a plastic bag, and chill. The lettuce will keep fresh for about a week. If the roots are disease-free, put them on the compost heap.

If you are growing American lettuces, harvest these like spinach by pulling off individual leaves from the outside of the plant when they are firm, but still young and tender. The plant will continue to produce new leaves for quite a long time.

Growing in containers

If you do not have a heated greenhouse, you can grow lettuces in containers indoors for winter supplies of fresh salad. Lettuces are a good vegetable to

Loose-leaf lettuces are ideal for growing in individual pots on a sunny windowsill. Pick leaves as required.

grow in containers, as there are several dwarf varieties available. Cabbage lettuces which require a lot of space are unsuitable, so choose from the smaller varieties available or plant cos or the loose-leaf American types. Tom Thumb lettuce, a cabbage type specially bred for small gardens or containers, needs only 15 cm (6") when mature and will grow well in 20 cm (8") plant pots.

Sow the seeds in containers, tubs or individual pots filled with a good quality compost. Sow about 7.5 cm (3") apart and cover with a fine layer of compost, or with compost mixed with peat. If you have the space for several containers, make successional sowings to extend the period of cutting. Thin the 5 cm (2") high seedlings to a distance of 15 cm (6") apart for loose-leaf varieties and 20 cm (8") apart for cos types. If you use individual pots, sow about 3 seeds to each one, and then thin to the strongest seedling.

Keep your containers in a warm sunny position, and remember that all lettuces need a great deal of water and the soil must never be allowed to dry out.

Cut your lettuces as soon as they have hearted, or pull off mature leaves from the American types. When one plant is cut, you can replant new seed in the same pot and have a succession of lettuces.

Varieties

There are hundreds of varieties of lettuces available to the home grower, a vast selection of different types for sowing at different seasons. Consider what type of lettuce you prefer, and plan your succession of sowings according to season. Some seed merchants offer lettuce variety packs containing seeds of several types to be sown throughout the year. We have divided our list of selected varieties into cabbage, cos and loose-leaf American types, and we have indicated under each variety the best time for sowing.

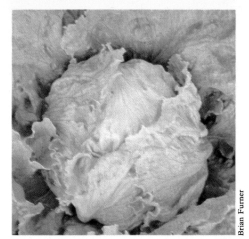
Webb's Wonderful

Cabbage lettuces (summer and autumn varieties)

All the Year Round: butterhead; good for sowing throughout the year, but does best in spring or autumn sowings; crisp, well-flavoured lettuces.

Appia: quick-maturing, high-quality lettuces; excellent for mid-summer sowings because it is resistant to mildew.

Webb's Wonderful: one of the most consistently popular and reliable of the crispheart types; large heads with well-flavoured crinkly leaves; slow to run to seed even in hot, dry weather.

Great Lakes: high-quality crisphead which makes large, solid hearts; slow to bolt; one of the best varieties for areas with hot summers.

Great Lakes

Windermere: smaller, earlier, more compact version of *Great Lakes;* also slow to run to seed in hot weather; good choice for a small garden.

Tom Thumb: the smallest variety; well flavoured butterheads; needs only 15 cm (6″) when mature; ideal for small gardens, frames or containers.

Buttercrunch: popular butterhead; small, dark green heads with creamy yellow central heart; keeps better than most types.

Avondefiance: dark green butterhead for early or mid-summer sowing; resistant to mildew and root aphid.

Tom Thumb

Ilo New!: excellent new variety which is highly disease-resistant and slow to bolt; crisp, sweet butterhead with yellow hearts; sow in succession from early spring.

Ballerina: new variety similar to Great Lakes; neat and compact crisphead; can be grown closer together than most varieties; slow to bolt.

Cabbage lettuces (winter and spring varieties)

Artic King: good for autumn sowing; small, compact heads with pale green, crumpled leaves.

Imperial Winter: extremely hardy; one of the largest varieties for autumn sowing; very reliable.

Valdor: excellent, very large winter lettuce; crisp, solid, deep green hearts; resistant to cold, wet conditions, so good for autumn sowing; new introduction.

Kordaat: one of the best varieties for greenhouse sowing; produces lettuces throughout the winter.

Kwiek: large-headed variety for greenhouse growing; sow in early autumn for crisp, well-flavoured lettuces in early winter.

May Queen: cut in early spring from early autumn greenhouse sowing; small heads; pale green leaves with slight pink tinge.

Premier: sow under glass in mid-autumn or mid-winter for transplanting outdoors in mid-spring; early variety; fairly large green heads.

Hilde: pale green, compact, smooth-leaf heads; early hearting; not prone to bolt; good for frame or outdoor sowing to crop in summer.

National Vegetables Research Station

Arctic King

Harry Smith

Amanda

Brian Furner

Hilde

44

Amanda: quick growing variety for greenhouse or frame; makes heavy, solid hearts.

Ramcos: new variety which is very disease-resistant; good for forcing in a cool or heated greenhouse; quick maturing; small enough for a windowbox.

Cos lettuces

Lobjoits Green Cos: very large heads; self-folding crisp leaves over dark green hearts; suitable for spring or autumn sowing; slow to bolt.

Little Gem: dwarf, compact, very early cos; crisp, bright green leaves; sow outdoors from early spring to midsummer; also succeeds under cloches; one of the best flavoured lettuces.

Winter Density: hardy; successful for autumn, spring or early summer sowing; dwarf and compact; very crisp with green hearts.

Lobcross: new variety to harvest in autumn; grows well in most conditions; very solid and well flavoured.

Paris White: noted for its resistance to bolting; very large cos with self-folding leaves; crisp and sweet.

Island Cos: thick and fleshy very dark green leaves; yellowish hearts.

Loose-leaf American lettuces

Salad Bowl: the best of the loose-leaf varieties; deeply curled green leaves resemble endive; large with crisp and tender leaves; does not bolt; sow outdoors from mid-spring to midsummer; excellent for containers.

Grand Rapids: tasty non-heading lettuce for greenhouse growing; will also grow outdoors from spring or summer.

Harry Smith

Lobjoits Green Cos

Brian Furner

Little Gem

Pat Brindley

Salad Bowl

45

Pests & Diseases

Lettuces can be bothered by a number of pests and diseases and, although most of them are not serious, precautions should be taken to ensure a healthy crop.

Lettuce root aphids: lettuce root aphids can attack the roots and collars of growing plants, causing the lettuces to turn yellow, wilt and rapidly decay. Different varieties have different levels of susceptibility. Attacks are most serious in late summer, and can be a particular problem in dry weather, when the moisture content in the plants is already low. The roots appear yellow and covered with a white woolly substance. The flies will be attracted to any decaying lettuces in the area, so pull out and burn any lettuce stumps or remains of plants. Lettuce rows should be hoed regularly to destroy weeds which could act as hosts to the pests. A dressing of naphthalene at 60 g per sq m (2 oz per sq yd) or watering between the rows with diluted derris in early summer are useful precautions.

Eelworm: eelworms (nematodes) are microscopic creatures which attack the roots of lettuces, producing small knobs on them and weakening the plants severely. The lettuces wilt and die. Destroy any affected plants immediately, and do not grow lettuces on the same ground for at least five years, as the eggs can remain there dormant.

Lettuce root maggot: this maggot, also called the chrysanthemum root maggot, causes severe injury to the roots of lettuces and chrysanthemums. The flies lay their eggs in the soil near lettuces, and the small, yellowish maggots hatch out and bore into the roots, causing the plants to wilt and die. Lettuces should never be grown too close to chrysanthemums, and never on the same ground. Reduce egg-laying by dusting around the base of the lettuces with flake naphthalene at weekly in-

Plants with mottled yellow leaves and stunted growth—the symptoms of mosaic virus.

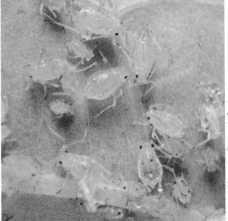

Greenfly attack lettuces in spring, checking growth and spreading diseases.

Grey mould fungus causes the lettuce stem to blacken and the roots to rot away.

tervals in late spring and early summer. Maggots can be killed by watering with a solution of g-BHC applied according to the manufacturer's instructions. However, it is better to prevent an attack of flies than to try and deal with the maggots.

Greenfly: both young and mature lettuces are at risk from greenfly attacks. The flies swarm on young summer lettuces in mid to late spring, checking growth and preventing them from hearting. Attacks are usually worse in a dry spring, as there is no rain to wash off the flies. Older plants can also be attacked, whether grown outdoors or in a greenhouse. Prevent greenfly attacks by spraying with a non-poisonous spray, such as pyrethrum, in spring. A fumigated greenhouse should be free of aphids, but if any are seen then spray the plants. Never put infested plants on the compost heap.

Slugs: as with all leafy crops, slugs are a menace to lettuces. They eat holes through the leaves and can quickly destroy a crop. Destroy slugs with methiocarb or methaldehyde baits.

Grey mould: grey mould fungus is the most common problem a lettuce grower will encounter, and you can easily identify it by the grey mouldy spots found on the leaves. The disease can attack plants at all stages of growth, and the result is always rapid decay. The disease usually enters the stem at soil level, often through a dead outer leaf, or through yellowing seed leaves in young plants. Carefully remove any bits of dead or dying leaves from lettuces and, if the disease appears, remove and destroy any infected plants, along with the soil from around their roots. Spraying with dichlofluanid or benomyl according to the packet instructions can be quite effective. Under glass, if grey mould has been a problem sterilize the soil six weeks before sowing by watering with a formalin solution.

Downy mildew: certain varieties of lettuces are subject to downy mildew, often seen as whitish spots on the leaves

GUIDE TO LETTUCE TROUBLES	
Symptom	Probable cause
Wilting, dying plants	Lettuce root aphids
	Eelworm
	Lettuce root maggot
Yellowing roots covered in white wool	Lettuce root maggot
Larva in seed	Lettuce seed fly
Holes in leaves	Slugs
	Ring spot
Mouldy grey spots on leaves	Grey mould
White spots on leaves	Downy mildew
	Ring spot
Brown patches on leaves	Bacterial spot
Mottled yellow leaves	Mosaic virus

of overcrowded seedlings, or on mature plants. To prevent, thin seedlings at an early stage, regulate watering and ventilation under glass. Zineb or thiram sprays applied according to the manufacturer's instructions give quite effective control.

Mosaic virus disease: greenfly spread mosaic virus disease of lettuces, which produces yellow mottled leaves and stunts the growth of plants. The infection can also be carried in the seed, so be sure your seed is certified clean. There is no cure for mosaic virus disease: burn infected plants and destroy any greenfly with pyrethrum.

Leaf spot disease: lettuces can be affected by several leaf spot diseases. Bacterial spot causes browning of the leaves along the veins and at the edges. Autumn lettuces which have been heavily manured or over-watered and those grown under glass are most often affected. Maintain a careful balance of moisture to avoid this disease.

Ring spot is a fungus disease sometimes seen in cold, damp weather. It starts as brown spots on leaves, and the spots turn white and fall out, leaving big holes. The lettuces are quickly made unusable. Good ventilation in frame or greenhouse will discourage the disease, and crop rotation will lessen attacks outdoors. Destroy infected plants.

Mushrooms

Agaricus bisporus (fam. *Agaricaceae*)
Capped fungus
Sowing to harvesting time: 4-12
weeks; the harvest then continues for
11-12 weeks longer.
Size: mushrooms up to 7.5 cm (3″) high; caps vary from
about 2.5 cm (1″) across for button mushrooms to 10 cm
(4″) across for mature ones.
Yield: at least 0.45-1.0 kg (1-2 lb) per sq m (sq yd); can be
much higher, depending on the quality of compost.

One of the most popular foods, mushrooms are different in character, shape, and method of cultivation from other vegetables. They are widely grown commercially, but mushrooms can easily be cultivated on a smaller scale by the home grower. Mushrooms are expensive in the shops all through the year, and it is much more economical to grow them yourself, as the initial outlay is quite small. A second point in favour of homegrown mushrooms is that mushrooms are at their best when freshly picked; they quickly lose their flavour and become tough and stale. The best guarantee that the mushrooms are fresh is to harvest them yourself just before cooking. A third point is that you can superintend the ingredients and making of the growing medium yourself, and so choose materials for the compost which will ensure the same rich flavour in your home-grown mushrooms that the wild field mushroom has. In the kitchen, mushrooms can be used whole or chopped, and eaten raw in salads or cooked by almost any method. Most of the work in growing mushrooms is

connected with the preparation of the special compost in which they grow; after the compost has been prepared, very little is needed in the way of cultivation and care.

Botanically, mushrooms are the fruiting bodies of the fungus *Agaricus bisporus*. The entire growth above the ground is edible; it consists of a white, creamy or brownish cap on a brownish stalk. Mushrooms change shape slightly as they mature. Young mushrooms first appear as white pinheads on the surface of the mushroom bed; they develop short stalks as the buttons, or caps, grow larger. At this stage the caps are spherical in shape and the gills are covered with a membrane, or veil, which is connected to the stalk. As the mushroom matures, the stalk grows longer and the cap grows larger and begins to flatten out. The membrane tears as the cap expands, and exposes the brownish gills beneath.

The usual method of propagation is by spores, which are produced in the gills and correspond to the seeds of green plants. Because the brownish black

48

Although they are cultivated differently from other vegetables, mushrooms are easy, quick, and very economical to grow. Well-established beds will crop for several months.

Grant Heilman

powdery spores are microscopic in size and difficult to germinate except under special conditions, mushrooms are normally grown from spawn. Spawn, or mycelium, is the germ tube produced by the spores; each appears as a long, thread-like white filament. The spawn absorbs food and moisture from the compost and eventually produces the fruiting bodies, or mushrooms, which are then cropped.

Cultivated mushrooms are closely related to the edible wild mushrooms (*Agaricus campestris*) found in summer and autumn in fields and meadows. A word of warning, however: there are several species of wild mushrooms which are highly poisonous, and very similar in appearance to those which are edible. Unless you are fully knowledgeable about mushrooms, and can identify them accurately, it is best not to pick wild mushrooms for eating.

Suitable sites

Mushrooms are grown commerically in purpose-built mushroom houses and artificial caves, but the home grower should be able to find a suitable site, either indoors or out, for growing smaller crops of mushrooms. The main factors in growing mushrooms

When mushrooms are harvested at a young stage, they are called 'buttons'; as they mature they expand into 'cups' and, finally, 'opens', or 'flats'.

button

button

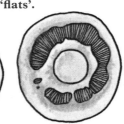

cup

open, or flat

successfully, besides suitable compost, are stable air temperature and moisture; you must select a site where these can be controlled. Indoors, you can use the floor of a cellar or shed; outdoors, they can be grown in greenhouses, cold frames or, in mild areas, in the open. Wherever they are grown, it is probably most convenient if you use boxes, other than beds, to contain the compost, remembering that boxes have the disadvantage of being wasteful of space.

If you are growing them in a shed or cellar, it must be clean, waterproof and dark. It is a good idea to disinfect old buildings before attempting to use them for mushroom growing, and dust the floor with lime as an additional precaution. It will be much easier to regulate the temperature inside a building if it is insulated; mushrooms will not grow if the temperature rises above 27°C (80°F) or falls below 7°C (45°F). There should also be some form of ventilation, so that the air can circulate freely. You can grow your mushrooms in wooden boxes or trays, with a depth of about 20 cm (8″) and any convenient size. You can also make up ridges directly on the floor, each about 45 cm (1½′) deep, and with a base of 60 cm (2′), rounding the top of the ridge. Or you can use a flat bed about 20-25 cm (8-10″) deep, but make it convenient for picking.

You can grow mushrooms in your greenhouse from mid-autumn through to mid-spring, if it is heated; under the staging is the best place to grow them, putting the compost either in boxes or directly on the greenhouse floor. They can also be grown on the staging, in containers; you will have to shade the glass fairly heavily as mushrooms become brown when exposed to sunlight, or make some arrangement to cover the containers or bed so as to exclude the light to some extent.

Outdoors, mushrooms can be grown in frames which are fairly deep; you will need a depth of at least 45 cm (1½′), though 60 cm (2′) is better. This allows a depth of compost of between 30 and 45 cm (1-1½′) and also gives reasonable conditions in which to keep the right temperature and humidity and allow the mushrooms room to grow. Lights will also be needed, and mats to shade the growing mushrooms. In very mild areas, mushrooms will grow outdoors on ridges from late winter through early summer and again from early autumn through late autumn. Make the ridges 60-75 cm (24-30″) wide and 45 cm (18″) high, and as long as is suitable. You can have them higher but not lower, since less good results will be obtained. You will need a good supply of straw and plastic sheeting in case of heavy, prolonged rain.

You can also grow mushrooms in a lawn or field. This is a chancy method, but can sometimes produce successful results. Simply lift a piece of turf in late

You can grow good mushroom crops on ridges outdoors in mild areas. Make ridges 60-75 cm (2′ 6″) wide, 45 cm (1′ 6″) high, and as long as is suitable.

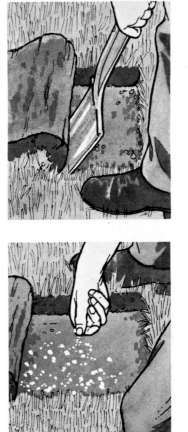

1. Lift a section of turf in late summer, when soil is moist and air warm and humid.

2. Using a small fork, loosen the exposed soil.

3. Scatter the spawn on the surface, then replace the turf and firm lightly.

4. The first flush should appear about a month later, depending on weather and soil conditions.

summer and place the spawn beneath it. The soil should be moist, and the atmosphere warm and humid. A touch of frost will not damage outdoor grown mushrooms. Finally, it is possible nowadays to buy mushroom kits which take the backbreak out of mushroom cultivation. They consist of a bucket containing prepared compost, which has already been spawned; you simply add water to start the spawn growing, carry out a few other simple instructions and pick mushrooms a few weeks later.

Compost preparation
As it is important to know the temperature of the compost during the various stages of making it, you should obtain a soil thermometer.

The easiest way to grow small crops of mushrooms is to buy mushroom kits. These buckets contain prepared spawn and compost, plus instructions for growing and harvesting the crop.

Manure being prepared for compost is stacked in a heap and kept moist by watering.

Mushrooms are usually grown on a compost made from strawy horse manure. Other materials can be used, such as pig or cow manure or any animal manure; wheat straw with fertilizer added has been tried and is much used commercially, also barley or bean straw, and bracken, again with the addition of nutrients. If you are making compost from horse manure, make sure it is fresh and has not been exposed to the weather for a long time. You should begin preparing the compost about a month before it is needed. Stack the manure in piles about 1.2 m (4′) high. This can be done outdoors in the summer; otherwise the stacking must be done in a shed or similar building to protect the manure from wet weather. If it is at all dry, water the manure; it should be moist but not really wet. If it is almost pure dung, without much litter, add wheat straw in the proportions of 1 part straw to 10 of dung (by volume) and mix thoroughly. Leave the stack alone for about seven days, during which time it will begin to

ferment; the temperature inside it should be in the region of 65°C (150°F). This will kill all insect pests and should destroy most fungal diseases. Once it has reached this temperature, you can turn it, putting the manure that was on the outside into the centre of the new heap, and breaking up all lumps as you proceed. Shake it at the same time to aerate it. Turn the stack another four or five times, at about four-day intervals, moistening the manure if it is at all dry. In about three to four weeks time, the compost should be brown, crumbly and moist, with the straw still recognisable but only just, and there should no longer be a smell of ammonia. It will now have a temperature of about 27°C (80°F) and is ready for use. Commercial growers often add gypsum, at the rate of about 0.45 kg (1 lb) gypsum to 40 kg (88 lb) manure compost—during the first turn—to prevent the finished product from being excessively sticky.

When horse manure is unavailable, you can use other animal manures as a substitute, ready-made mushroom compost, or home-made compost. The latter is made with the aid of an activator. A proprietary brand of this chemical can be bought from your seedsman or garden shop. Specific instructions will be provided, but the general principle is simple. Make a heap with alternate layers of straw or any other similar materials suggested, and activator and then follow the same procedure outlined for manure. The heap must also be kept moist but not wet.

Spawning and casing

The spawn, generally shaped into fibrous blocks (though now also available in granular form) can be bought from seedsmen or garden centres. For the spawning of your mushrooms, you need an air temperature of about 21°C (70°F); after covering it can be dropped to about 15°C (60°F). Mushrooms will grow at any temperature above 10°C (50°F), but more slowly at the lower temperatures. Too high temperatures can kill the spawn. This is, of course, more easily maintained within a building than outdoors.

When filling boxes or trays put the compost in firmly, but not packed down hard so that air is completely excluded. Beds and ridges should similarly be

PREPARING COMPOST

1. Build manure stack about a month before compost is needed; spray with water to promote fermentation, but do not soak.

2. Use a fork to turn the heap four or five times every few days to ensure it rots evenly and stays moist. When ready, it should be brown, moist and crumbly.

INDOOR CULTIVATION

1. Test the soil and plant spawn when temperature falls to 21°C (70°F).

2. Break walnut-sized pieces of spawn from the cake and plant them 2.5 cm (1") deep and 20-25 (8-10") apart.

packed firmly and evenly, but not trodden—disease can come in on footwear. Ridge beds, which give slightly higher yields from the same floor space, are usually made in pairs. Make the base of the ridges 60 cm (2') wide, gently tapering at the top to 15 cm (6"). Height should be 45 cm (1½') from top to base.

When the compost has been put into position, its temperature will again rise, to about 38°C (100°F) and will then gradually fall. Keep the bed moderately well watered during this period—when squeezed, the compost should feel damp but should not drip water. After a few days, the temperature will fall to 21°C (70°F). This is the correct moment to

3. If using grain spawn, scatter it on surface; cover box with black plastic.

These rye grains have been impregnated with mushroom mycelium spawn.

Cake mushroom mycelium spawn is sold dry, and is activated by warmth and moisture.

54

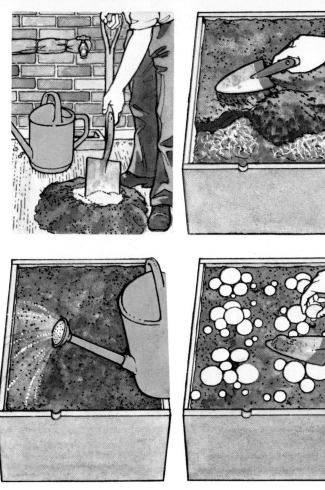

4. **Prepare casing of sterilized soil, or a mixture of peat and chalk or gypsum. Mix thoroughly.**

5. **Ten days after white threads of mycelium spawn appear, spread casing lightly over compost to a depth of 2.5 cm (1").**

6. **If the casing seems to be drying out, water sparingly; always keep box well ventilated.**

7. **Pull mushrooms from compost with a twist of the hand; do not cut.**

insert the spawn; if the temperature is lower, growth may be very slow.

Break the cake into fragments about the size of a walnut and insert pieces about 2.5 cm (1") deep in the compost, at a spacing of 20-25 cm (8-10") in each direction. Press the compost firmly around and over the spawn, so that no air pockets develop.

After a week or so, the mushroom mycelium will be seen spreading like fine greyish to white threads through and on the compost. Leave it for a further ten days, then cover it with a casing of fine, moist soil whose pH is between 7.0 and 8.0. The casing helps to retain the heat of the bed and also helps to conserve moisture. A fine, rich, loamy soil is ideal, and if it has been sterilized, so much the

better. Cover the compost evenly to a depth of 2.5 cm (1"). Alternatively, the casing can consist of a mixture of moist peat and chalk or gypsum, in the ratio of three to one by volume.

Care and development

The mushrooms should appear about two to three weeks after casing, according to the temperature. During this period water sparingly, and only if the casing seems to be drying out. If the beds are over-watered, and the manure beneath the casing is drenched, the spawn will be killed. If, on the other hand, the beds are too dry, the spawn will grow away from the surface of the bed, and deeper into the compost, with the result that no mushrooms will appear

Commercially, mushrooms are cultivated on shelves in purpose-built mushroom houses.

on the surface of the soil. Ideally, the casing should be kept moist with lukewarm water, applied as a fine spray. During this time, the temperature of the bed must not be allowed to rise above 21°C (70°F) for more than brief periods, or the mycelium will be damaged. On the other hand, it should not become cool, and it is a good idea to cover outdoor beds or ridges with a layer of loose straw up to 45 cm (1½') thick, depending on the time of year. Keep the beds well ventilated, but avoid draughts. The air around a mushroom bed should be moist but also fresh.

Harvesting and aftercare

One to two months is the normal span of time from spawning to cropping, but it can sometimes take longer. If the manure has not fermented properly, or there is inadequate moisture or heat at

any time, it may take up to twelve weeks for the mushrooms to be ready.

The developing mushrooms appear directly over the spawn, so the crops should be evenly distributed over the surface of the bed. Mushrooms tend to reach maturity all at the same time, in 'spates', or 'flushes'. When the first flush is ready for picking,' twist out each mushroom and break it off from the cluster. You should clean out the stem bases from the compost as you pick the mushrooms, to avoid infections and infestations gaining a hold on the beds. After this routine cleaning, fill the holes in the bed with fresh soil. Water the bed thoroughly, although not to the point of saturation. A second flush should appear in about ten days.

Cropping will continue for about three months. If the bed stops cropping prematurely, give it an additional thorough watering. This is often all that is needed to start production again.

Beds in production will need a good steady supply of water as long as cropping continues; make sure that the temperature of the water is the same as the temperature of the bed.

When the last of the mushrooms have been gathered, the compost should be immediately cleared. Never use any of the old compost and soil for growing mushrooms again, although it makes excellent manure for other crops. Give the frames, boxes or other containers a thorough disinfecting to remove any traces of insects or infections. You should also lime-wash the walls and scrub the floors.

Exhibition tips

Timing mushrooms for a particular show date can be a bit risky; mushrooms can be ready for harvesting from one to two months after the spawn has been planted. To avoid disappointment, prepare a small mushroom bed two months before the show, another six weeks before, and a third bed a month before the show date.

Mushrooms can either be shown as buttons, with the gills still covered by the membranes and not visible, or as cups, when the gills are open but have not yet fully expanded. Twelve is the usual number required, either as single exhibits or as part of a collection of vegetables. Because mushrooms deteriorate rapidly once they are picked, delay the picking until the last possible moment. Pick more than you need for the exhibit, so you will have replacements at the show bench, should they be necessary. Whether they are shown as cups or buttons, they should be as uniform as possible.

There is very little pre-show preparation needed. Simply trim the stems to a uniform length of 2.5 cm (1″). At the show, the mushrooms can be displayed in a shallow basket, box or tray. They will look best displayed near the front of the staging.

Varieties

There is only one kind of mushroom available to the amateur grower; this is the species *Agaricus bisporus*. Commercial names attached to mushroom spawn only indicate the particular firm which has produced and marketed the spawn.

Pests & Diseases

White mould (Bubbles): this is a fungal disease which covers the mushrooms with white mouldy growths; the gills are particularly vulnerable to infection, and a badly attacked mushroom may simply be a rounded mass, completely covered with the mould. In very bad attacks, whole clumps of young mushrooms can be enveloped in white mould and killed. Because white mould usually enters the beds in the casing soil, the best precaution is to use only peat or sterilized soil. Once an attack of white mould has occurred, remove and burn all infected mushrooms and stumps immediately. After the final crop, spray the containers and the inside of the building or greenhouse with a solution of formalin, or zineb.

White plaster mould: this is another fungal infection, which shows up on the surface of the beds as a pale powdery growth much like a top dressing of lime in appearance. It prevents the growth of the mushrooms and usually appears as a result of improper composting of the manure. It is favoured by alkaline conditions; the use of gypsum in the compost will generally prevent its appearance. If the beds have suffered from white plaster mould, disinfect the containers or building after the final crop.

Brown plaster mould: a relatively minor fungal infection, this appears on the surface of the bed first as a white fluffy patch. In a few days, the centre of the white patch will turn brown;

The fungal disease white mould, or bubbles, covers mushrooms with white, mouldy growth.

These brown, sticky mushrooms display the symptoms of brown blotch infection.

eventually, the whole fungus turns brown and powdery. As with white plaster mould, improper composting is the main cause. Hygienic conditions and properly made compost will help to prevent its appearance.

Brown blotch: this bacterial infection makes the caps brown, sticky and inedible. Because it thrives in warm, moist still air, proper ventilation and moderate watering can avoid it.

Mushroom bed sclerotium: if you find branch-shaped, hardened growths in the casing soil, often with pinkish tips showing just above the soil surface, then your beds are infected with mushroom bed sclerotium. Pull them out of the soil and destroy them; you should still be able to harvest good crops.

Dry bubble: light brown spots and blotches appear on the mushroom cap, and later the mushrooms become distorted and the stalks split and peel. They become dry and leathery in time. Treat as for white mould; chlorinated water is also helpful.

Cobweb disease: a downy or fluffy mould appears on the compost surface and grows all over the mushrooms also, which then rot completely. Sometimes the mould has a pinkish tinge. Treat as for white mould.

Rose comb: the symptoms of this physiological disorder are deformed or cracked caps. Often gills are produced on top of the caps. Rose comb is caused by exposing the beds to fumes from oil stoves, or by applying mineral-based sprays.

Woodlice: these pests thrive in the humidity, darkness and decaying manure which are necessary for growing mushrooms. Once they enter the beds, either with the manure or else through cracks or holes in the shed, they will multiply rapidly. They eat holes in the developing buttons, and in severe infestations the entire crop can ruined. Gamma-HCH or pyrethrum applied to the bed are the best methods of control.

Slugs: slimy, silvery trails on the surface of the bed and ragged holes in the buttons indicate the presence of slugs. Hand pick if possible, at night when they feed, or trap them with proprietary slug baits as soon as they are seen, but put the bait near to the beds or boxes, rather than on them, as slug baits are poisonous to humans also.

Springtails: these tiny jumping insects often appear in great numbers and can do an enormous amount of damage. They attack the stalks, gills and outer edges of the caps, which then become slightly pitted. Once they have attacked the developing buttons, no further growth takes place, and the crops will be severely stunted. Compost which has heated up to the temperature recommended should not be troubled, but spraying or dusting the growing medium with gamma-HCH, pyrethrum or derris should control an infestation.

Sciarid flies: these tiny black gnats lay

58

The physiological disorder rose comb appears as extra gills growing on top of the caps.

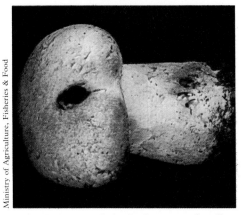

Mites have eaten holes in the cap and stalk of this mushroom; control is difficult.

eggs on the surface of the compost and at the base of the mushroom stalks. The emerging tiny legless larvae, which are white with black heads, enter the base of the stalk and tunnel upwards; infected mushrooms decay. Treatment is the same as for springtails. High temperature composting in the first place will destroy larvae.

Mites: there are several species of mites which attack mushrooms, all of which eat internal holes in the stalks and caps. Unfortunately, mites have developed a resistance to most organochlorine-based insecticides, but derris or pyrethrum offer some measure of control. If the infestation is severe, the only completely effective method of control is to clear out all the beds, discard all the soil and manure, and disinfect the walls and floor of the shed with boiling water.

Phorid flies: these are similar to sciarid flies, and both insects do much the same damage. Phorid flies, however, are active mainly in the summer months, while sciarid flies occur all year round. The best preventive measure against phorid flies is to cover all ventilators, doors and windows with fine mesh screening. If an infestation does occur, spray or dust the beds with derris or pyrethrum.

GUIDE TO MUSHROOM PROBLEMS

Symptoms	Probable cause
Holes eaten in buttons	Woodlice
Ragged holes in mushrooms; slimy trails on casing	Slugs
Pitted stalks, gills and outer caps	Springtails
Tunnels in stalk, decayed mushrooms	Sciarid flies Phorid flies
Holes eaten inside stalks and caps	Mites
White mouldy growths on mushrooms	White mould (Bubbles)
White powdery mould on casing	White plaster mould
White fluffy patches on casing, later turning brown	Brown plaster mould
Caps turn brown	Brown blotch
Pink tipped, branch-like growths in casing soil	Mushroom bed sclerotium
Light brown spots on cap, later distortions of mushroom and splitting of stalk	Dry bubble
White downy or fluffy mould on compost and mushrooms, sometimes pinkish	Cobweb disease
Deformed, cracked caps; gills on top	Rose comb

Peppers

Capsicum annuum, C. frutescens (fam. *Solanaceae*)
Annual or perennial, but most culinary capsicums are
grown as **half-hardy annuals.**
Sowing to harvesting time: 20–28 weeks
Size: plants vary in height from 30–90 cm (1–3′). Fruit of
dwarf varieties about 2.5 cm (1″) across; large varieties from
7.5–12 cm (3–5″) long.
Yield: 0.45–1 kg (1–2 lb) per plant.

Originally a native of tropical America,
peppers are becoming increasingly
popular as a flavourful vegetable cooked
in stews and casseroles, or served fresh in
salads. Widely grown in southern
Europe and warmer areas of the United
States, recent developments of F₁ hybrid
strains have made growing peppers in
cooler temperate climates possible; they
are now grown commercially in parts of
southern England.

Peppers have much to recommend
them; their bright red, green or yellow
colour and flavour add zest to any meal.
They are relatively expensive to buy in
the shops, but the home grower can
produce healthy-sized crops with little
initial expense. In good years, when
crops are abundant, excess peppers can
be frozen or dried and stored like onions.
Unlike tomatoes, which are virtually
inedible in their unripe state, unripe
peppers are very tasty, and indeed
preferred by some people to the milder,

sweeter ripe pepper. Unripe peppers are
dark green, and brilliant red or yellow
when ripe.

Peppers are relatively pest and disease
free, and their cultivation requirements
are few. Rich growing medium, warmth
and a steady water supply are necessary,
but they require no training, tying or
pinching out of sideshoots.

Peppers, besides their food value,
make very decorative pot plants; they
can be grown indoors and stood out on a
balcony, windowsill or paved courtyard
during the summer months. In a
greenhouse, they have much the same
growing requirements as tuberous be-
gonias; a mixed display of flowering
plants and bushes hung with peppers can
be very attractive.

There are many varieties available
from seed catalogues, some of which
have inedible fruits and are grown solely
for decorative value. The two main
categories of edible peppers are sweet

Chilli plants are very decorative as well as useful. The vivid, bright red hanging fruits which adorn the branches are visually attractive; when dried they are ground into chilli powder or cayenne pepper. These spices are used in the making of curry powder, pickles and tabasco sauce.

Derek Fell

peppers (*Capsicum annuum*) and hot peppers, or chillies (*Capsicum frutescens*). Sweet peppers, also called bullnose, bell or pimiento peppers, generally have larger fruit than chillies. The paprika made from these is much used in Hungarian cooking. The taste of peppers in general varies greatly in intensity, depending on ripeness and variety; some are sweet and mild, while others can be incredibly pungent. The peppery flavour is due to the presence of a chemical compound, capsicin, in the fruit; the more capsicin, the hotter the flavour. All peppers have a very high vitamin C content. The shape, size and texture varies; they can be round, oblong or conical in shape, wrinkled or smooth skinned, and from 5–15 cm (2–6″) long.

The small, tapering fruits, about 2.5 cm (1–2″) long of the *C. frutescens* types are renowned for their strong 'hot' flavour. Because of their pungency, these peppers are mostly used for flavouring only, the bright red flesh being dried and ground into chilli powder or cayenne pepper, or shredded. When green, chillies are pickled or made into chilli vinegar. Because they are so intensely flavoured, though, most households need only one plant to keep well supplied with chillies.

Suitable site

Peppers are tropical in origin, and will be killed by frost. For this reason, they are most successfully grown in greenhouses, either in pots or in the border under

**In mild sheltered
areas, peppers
can be grown
outside, at the
base of a south-
facing wall. In
early summer,
transplant
peppers started
under glass to a
growing-bag
outside.**

**Alternatively, in
early summer
plunge the pots
containing the
pepper plants up
their rims in a
sunny border.
Lift them in
autumn, and
return the pots
to the
greenhouse to
finish ripening.**

staging. In very mild, sheltered areas, peppers can be started under glass and planted outside in early summer, against a south facing wall. New F_1 varieties have been bred for hardiness, and growing peppers out of doors is certainly less risky than it used to be. A late frost, however, can still be disastrous. Cloche protection lessens the risk somewhat, but because strong growing pepper plants are taller than most cloches, the cloches will have to be raised to accommodate them.

You can combine the advantages of greenhouse and outdoor cultivation: start the plants in a greenhouse, and in early summer, plunge the pots up to the rims in sunny borders outdoors. They will then have the benefit of the hot summer months. When summer is over and autumn comes, lift the pots from the borders outdoors, and bring them into the greenhouse. Here they will be able to ripen off in the warmer atmosphere.

Suitable soil

Outdoors, and in the greenhouse border, peppers thrive in rich, well worked soil containing plenty of manure. For growing in pots, standard

1. Begin sowing seeds from late winter onwards. Space seeds 2.5 cm (1″) apart in all directions in the tray.

2. At the three-leaf stage, prick the seedlings out into 7.5 cm (3″) pots and lower the temperature slightly.

3. Do not allow plants to become root bound; repot them into 12 cm (5″) pots and richer compost as necessary.

4. Harden plants off in a cold frame or under cloches prior to moving them outdoors into the open ground.

potting composts, such as John Innes No 3, are suitable. Alternatively, use plastic growing bags filled with prepared compost, such as those used for tomatoes.

Sowing and planting out

The timing of sowing depends on whether the plants are to be grown entirely in a greenhouse, or a combination of greenhouse and out of doors. Seeds for greenhouse peppers can be sown in late winter or early spring; for plants intended for cloche or outdoor fruiting without protection, the beginning of mid-spring is the best time. You can sow peppers out of doors, either directly in the ground or in peat pots after the last frosts, in mild sheltered areas. Peppers need a long growing season, though, so it is really best to start them off in a warm greenhouse or propagator, or even in a warm room.

Sow the seeds in trays, spaced 2.5 cm (1″) apart in all directions, and push them about 1.3 cm (½″) below the surface of the compost. John Innes No 1 is the most suitable medium. Peat pots can also

FEEDING PEPPERS

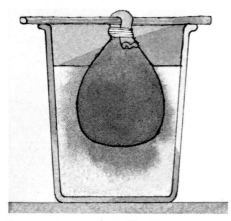

Prepare home-made liquid manure; dilute it to the colour of weak tea before feeding the plants.

Alternatively, buy liquid food and dilute according to manufacturer's instructions; feed while fruits form.

be used, sowing two or three seeds in each pot. A soil temperature of 18°C (65°F) is ideal, but seeds will still germinate if it drops a few degrees below this for short periods of time. The first leaves should be showing two to three weeks after sowing, depending on temperature.

When the seedlings reach the three-leaf stage, prick them out into 7.5 cm (3") pots. The temperature can be lowered now to 13°C (55°F) during the day dropping to 10°C (50°F) at night. Do not allow the plants to become root bound;

as they grow re-pot them into larger pots and richer compost to encourage the development of good growth. If they are to fruit indoors, use 15 cm (6") or 17.5 cm (7") pots for the final potting ; if they are to be planted outdoors, 12.5 cm (5") pots are large enough. In the early stages they are very slow to grow but, provided they remain a good colour, there is no need to worry.

Never move half-hardy pepper plants straight from a warm greenhouse or kitchen windowsill into the open garden. The plants should be hardened off gradually, until they are completely used to the lower outdoor temperature. Do this by putting them in a cold frame for a short period of time, or giving them cloche protection outdoors during the day, while they are still in their pots, and bringing them back to the greenhouse at night. After one or two weeks, the plants can be left out permanently.

It is safest to wait until the beginning of early summer before planting out permanently; do this about the same time as you plant out tomatoes under cloches. If the spring is exceptionally cold, delay planting out until the weather and soil warm up. Do not let the plants starve, though; if they have to remain in their pots longer because of cold weather, top dress with nitro-chalk and water it in.

Set out the young plants 37.5–60 cm (15–24") apart, depending on variety. Always water the soil well before planting unless it is already moist.

Cultivation and care
Peppers need a steady supply of water if their growth is not checked. If the soil becomes dry, even for a short period of time during mid-day, the plants will droop at once. The leaves, being thin, tend to dry up more quickly than most; syringing them daily in hot weather helps reduce transpiration, as well as keeping red spider mite away. A position where they are shaded from the late morning and mid-day sun is ideal especially when the plants are young.

1. If using peat pots, sow two or three seeds per pot; remove all but the strongest seedling.

2. If cold weather delays planting out, top-dress the plants with nitro-chalk and water in thoroughly.

3. Plant out in early summer when the weather warms up; the plants should be about 20 cm (8″) tall.

4. Give plants cloche protection at night or if weather turns cold; take cloches off during the day.

5. Peppers need plenty of water, particularly at mid-day in hot weather; their thin leaves dry out quickly.

6. Mulch with clean dry straw once the plants are established, to keep weeds down and conserve moisture.

Remember, though, to water steadily and moderately, because over-enthusiastic watering can lead to botrytis infections, especially in cool weather.

In very warm weather, provide some form of light shading, particularly to those grown under glass.

Peppers grown in pots respond well to liquid feeding once the fruits have begun to form, using a potash-high feed, and this can be done at routine watering times, applied according to manufacturers' instructions. Alternatively, you can make liquid manure by steeping a bag of rotted manure in a tub of water; use this after diluting it to the colour of weak tea and apply once a week.

If you have been thorough in preparing the soil for outdoor plants, you should have no trouble with perennial weeds. Any annual weeds which appear can be kept down with a hoe, worked between rows. Be careful not to damage the roots of the pepper plants; hand weeding plants is best. A mulch with clean straw, once the plants are established, will keep the weeds down, as well as conserving soil moisture.

Artificial pollination is not really necessary as the greenish-white flowers set fruit readily, and may indeed need thinning to get the best sized peppers. However, misting the plants daily while they are flowering improves the rate of pollination. Never grow sweet peppers and hot peppers in the same greenhouse, because the cross-pollination which may occur would have disastrous results.

You may need to give support, in the form of bamboo poles to the taller growing varieties; the dwarf kinds stand up well without support. Some people advise pinching out the growing tips when the plants are 20 cm (8") high, but eventually, when the plants are fully grown, there is little difference between plants treated in this way and those allowed to develop naturally.

Harvesting and aftercare

Peppers grown under glass should be ready for picking in mid-summer; if the

Peppers grown under glass will be ready for harvesting in mid-summer; those grown out of doors can be picked from late summer.

greenhouse is heated, harvesting should continue until early winter. Those grown outdoors will normally be ready for picking before late summer or early autumn, and harvesting will stop as soon as the weather turns cold. The length of the harvesting season depends to some extent on local climate, and can also vary from summer to summer. The fruits should be picked as soon as they are of sufficient size, and the flesh is firm and well filled out. A good quality pepper has a smooth pleasing shape and an even colour. Peppers taste delicious at all stages, and many people prefer them when they are still green and slightly under-ripe. Peppers left on the plant to ripen fully will turn a rich red or yellow, depending on variety; they are somewhat sweeter than the green ones.

In some varieties, the fruit hangs down from the shoots; in others, the peppers grow erect from the upper sides of the stems. Cut the fruit from the parent plant with a sharp knife or secateurs, leaving the remaining peppers, which develop at different rates, undisturbed. Handle the peppers carefully, so that they are not bruised. A

66

1. Pinch out the first few flowers by hand to encourage the formation of larger fruit. Keep well watered.

2. Prevent infestation by the pest red spider mite with a daily spray of water on the undersides of the leaves.

strong plant should produce between at least six and eight peppers. One word of warning, however: the peppers will remain in good condition on the plant for sometime after they are ripe, but if you do not pick them the production of additional peppers will cease. It is best to harvest peppers as soon as they are ready, except perhaps towards the end of the season, when the plant has finished forming fruits. Because peppers continue to flower over a long period, you are unlikely to be faced with a sudden glut of them. Any which are picked green in mid-autumn will ripen slowly until early or even mid-winter.

Hot peppers are picked in much the same way as sweet peppers; in their unripe state they are used for pickling, and when ripe, for drying and grinding into chilli powder. Fruit can be stored by threading string through the stalks and hanging them to dry in a cool place. If picked when green, for storage, they will gradually change colour until they are red or yellow.

Do not leave the plants in the soil after harvesting has been completed; in temperate climates they are treated as annuals and there is no point in keeping them longer. Pull up and burn or compost old plants. Remember never to put on the compost heap any plants showing signs of pests or diseases.

Exhibition tips

Because of their intensely bright colour, peppers and chillies will enliven any display, either on their own or as part of a collection. Although botanically fruit, the Royal Horticultural Society classifies them as vegetables for the purpose of exhibition. Although peppers are not worth as many points as some vegetables, it is not difficult to grow first class specimens to give you the maximum that are available. As they are extremely attractive, they are particularly useful for bringing colour to sombre displays.

Peppers can be displayed while they are still green, or when they have ripened fully and are red or yellow. This means that timing the date of sowing is not as tricky as it is with some other vegetables, which are at their best for a few days only. As general guide, sow under glass in early to mid-spring for late summer or early autumn shows.

If you particularly want to exhibit fully coloured peppers, and due to unforeseen weather changes it is unlikely that they will ripen naturally in time for the show, you can force ripening. A few days before the show, pick the peppers and wrap them individually in tissue paper. Pack them in a single layer in a box so that all light is excluded. Place the box in a warm room or greenhouse, and inspect the peppers daily. Take out any which have ripened and have begun to shrivel, and store them in a cool dark place until the show.

Twelve peppers is the usual number shown; because chillies are much smaller, twenty-four is the usual number required. Try to have double this amount ready for showing, so that you can select the best. Because peppers are by their very nature irregular and unsymmetrical in shape, it is unlikely you will find perfectly uniform specimens. Try to select fruits which are approximately the same size and colour, however, for the best visual effect.

Cut the peppers with secateurs, leaving a good sized stalk attached to the fruit. This stalk will come in handy if you are wiring the peppers to a display stand. They should not need much preparation; just wash them lightly and dry afterwards. If the pepper is left wet for any length of time, rot may set in and

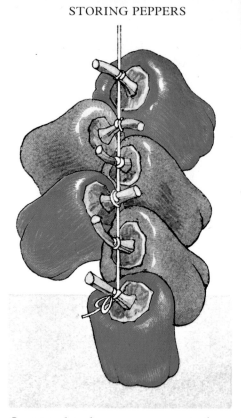

Sweet red and green peppers can be stored; thread a string through the stalks and hang in a dry place.

ruin your display.

If you are packing them for transport to the show, wrap them individually in tissue paper. Pack them tightly enough so they do not move about in the box and rub each other, or they may be bruised when you take them out.

Peppers can be displayed on plates or in shallow baskets, or wired to cones or other display shapes. If wiring them up, use tight bunches of parsley to fill the spaces between the peppers. Keep the parsley on short stalks and close to the wire form; if the parsley is loose or sloopy looking it will detract from the exhibit. Make sure you leave plenty of time to set up the exhibit before the show; chillies are particularly troublesome and time consuming to prepare because of their small size.

Varieties

Canapé (F₁): very early and suitable for outdoor cultivation; fruit sweet flavoured and bright red when ripe; heavy cropper.

Ace (F₁); new variety, early; heavy and uniform cropper; equally good for forcing or outdoor use; widely used commercially.

Californian Wonder: bull-nose type; forms large plants; mild, delicate flavour; this variety is good for deep freezing.

Worldbeater: well known variety; heavy cropper; fruits 12.5 cm (5″) long; skin dark green turning deep red when ripe; best grown under glass.

Emerald Gem: excellent taste; suitable for sheltered border outdoors or cultivation under glass.

Outdoor: blunt-nosed variety; red when fully ripe; half-hardy, needs cloches outdoors.

Slim Pim (F₁): small peppers, about 5 cm (2″) long with mild, sweet flavour; suitable for freezing; very heavy cropper; suitable for outdoor growing in mild areas.

Vinedale: very early variety; fruits mild, sweet, thick-fleshed and pointed; this variety does best in a warm sheltered position.

Bell Boy (F₁): new variety; heavy cropper; popular for commercial growing; this variety is excellent for home growing.

Novelty varieties

Tompa: similar to a tomato in shape and colour; juicier and sweeter than other peppers; suitable for growing in a greenhouse or close to a warm, south-facing wall.

Gold Topaz: unusual variety; peppers golden yellow when ripe, with mild, spicy flavour; best grown in cold frame or greenhouse.

Mexican Chilli: hot, spicy flavoured, small peppers; fruits dried and ground into chilli powder; must be grown in greenhouse.

Pests & Diseases

Capsid bugs: these bright green, quick-moving insects occasionally attack the growing points of pepper plants. They pierce the leaves and stems, and suck the sap, from mid-spring onwards. Infested leaves will be mis-shapen, puckered and tattered; infested growing points will be severely stunted or will die outright.

If your plants are attacked by capsids, which is unlikely, control them by spraying or dusting with malathion or derris plus pyrethrum. Capsids drop to the ground when disturbed, so remember to treat the ground around the plant as well.

Red spider mite: capsicums grown under glass seem particularly vulnerable to attacks by greenhouse red spider mite. The young and mature mites feed on the undersides of the leaves; the upper surfaces then become pale and speckled. If the attack is very bad, the leaves will turn yellow and fall prematurely. Leaves and stems covered with a fine web is another indication of red spider mite.

Because the insects are most destructive in hot, dry, overcrowded conditions, make sure your plants are properly spaced apart, with plenty of air circulation. Regular syringing, up to three times a day in very hot weather, is a good precaution. Use lukewarm water, and make sure both sides of the leaves are thoroughly dampened. If you find one or two leaves with a few mites on them, usually close to the main vein, removal of these leaves completely may well be enough to prevent any further outbreak.

If, however, there is a serious infestation, fumigation of the greenhouse with azobenzine will help control the pest. Alternatively, you can use derris or malathion as a spray. Red spider mites can develop a resistance to a particular chemical if it is used too frequently, so make sure you use insecticides according to manufacturers' instructions, and if there are no positive results after a couple of weeks, try another method of control.

G. E. Hyde

Whiteflies attack a wide range of plants; control with bioresmethrin.

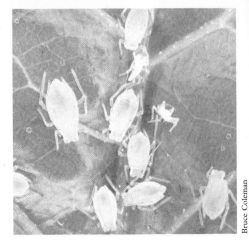

Bruce Coleman

Greenflies feed on the sap, resulting in yellow, puckered, curled leaves.

Botrytis (grey mould): this fungal infection attacks a wide variety of fruits and vegetables, and is usually associated with cool, damp, overcrowded conditions. Peppers grown under glass are particularly vulnerable. The disease can enter the plant through a wound or through dead or dying tissue. Because botrytis spores are present in the air, poor growing conditions can quickly lead to severe attack. The best precautions are to ensure that seedlings and young plants are not overcrowded, and that air can circulate freely. Quintozene applied to the soil just before planting gives some measure of protection. If there is an outbreak of botrytis, remove and burn all infected leaves and improve the growing conditions; badly infected plants should be removed and destroyed, as it is unlikely they will recover.

Whitefly: these insects, which look like small white moths, are more troublesome some years than others. They thrive in hot, dry weather, and whitefly attacks in these conditions can be severe. Like red spider mite, they live and feed on the undersides of leaves, where they suck the sap. They also exude honeydew, which encourages secondary infection from sooty mould. Spray with bioresmethrin as soon as they are seen, and again as necessary to destroy any newly hatched insects.

Greenfly: these are one of the many types of aphids which attack cultivated plants. Greenfly feed on the plant sap, the removal of which results in puckered, distorted and yellowed leaves, especially the young ones. Because greenfly breed rapidly, it is vital that you take action as soon as you see them. Spray with derris or malathion; repeat as necessary. In very severe cases, use a systemic insecticide, such as dimethoate. Remember to allow the recommended time to pass before harvesting the peppers.

GUIDE TO PEPPER TROUBLES

Symptom	*Probable cause*
Mis-shapen, puckered, tattered leaves	Capsids, greenfly, whitefly
Leaves pale, mottled, turn yellow and fall prematurely	Red spider mite
Leaves, fruits and stems covered in grey mould	Botrytis

Radishes

Raphanus sativus (fam. *Cruciferae*)
Hardy annual or biennial.
Sowing to harvesting time: three to six weeks for summer varieties, five months for winter varieties.
Size: varies with type, spring and summer radishes average 2.5 cm (1″) in diameter, winter radishes much larger, weighing up to 0.45 kg (1 lb) each.
Yield: 1.6 kg (4 lb) per 3 m (10′) row for summer varieties. 4.3 kg (10 lb) per 3 m (10′) row for winter varieties.

Radishes are one of the easiest and quickest vegetables to grow, giving a high yield of crisp roots with minimum effort. Because their cultivation needs are so few, and quick-growing varieties can be harvested three weeks after sowing, growing radishes is one of the best projects for children as an introduction to gardening. Radishes are, of course, an extremely useful crop in general; they can be sown between other plants, as catch crops, or in the odd corner of the garden. As long as the soil has been prepared properly and the plants do not run short of water, a good crop will be ready for pulling a short time after sowing. By giving some protection against the extremes of winter and summer weather, you can harvest good crops of radishes all year round.

Most commercially grown radishes, seen in the greengrocers in spring and summer, are the round red variety. The amateur gardener has a much wider selection of varieties from which to choose. Besides red radishes, there are white, yellow, red and white, and black-skinned types, round, long and tapering or oval in shape. Some varieties are suitable for early forcing, others are grown for autumn and winter harvesting. Packets of mixed strains are available; these contain seeds of several varieties of mixed colours, shapes and sizes. The different varieties of radish in these packets mature at different times, so the season of harvesting will be extended.

The most familiar types of radishes are the round red one and the slightly longer red and white type, which are popular for garnishing and for use in summer salads. These are sweeter-tasting than the long white variety, which has a peppery flavour and is also used in salads. The slower growing winter varieties form enormous roots, weighing up to about half a kilogramme (1 lb) each, and can be red or black-skinned, with white flesh. These are pungent and tasty, but not sweet. They can be cooked like turnips or eaten raw, in which case they are sliced or grated, rather than served whole. Winter varieties are peeled before eating but the summer varieties are eaten whole.

Summer radishes are quick growing and ready to pull three or four weeks after sowing.

Suitable site and soil

Success with radishes depends to a large extent on soil conditions. The soil must be rich and moist; warm, light fertile sandy soil is best. As with most other root crops, manuring the soil right before sowing is not a good practice, as it leads to coarse, badly shaped roots. You can lighten heavy clay soil by adding peat. Very dry soil can also be improved by the addition of peat, which increases the moisture-holding capacity of the soil. Whatever the soil type, it should be deeply dug well before sowing, and worked to a very fine tilth. There should be no lumps in the top 15 cm (6″) of soil. Work in sifted leafmould or ripe sifted garden compost, and add a dressing of bonemeal at the rate of 120 g per sq m (4 oz per sq yd).

Site requirements vary according to the time of year. For early outdoor sowings, a warm, sunny sheltered site is best, preferably with a south-facing slope. From early summer onwards, radishes need a cool, shady position. If they are grown in full sun during the summer months, they tend to bolt, or run to seed. Do not, however, plant them in a dry, shady place, such as under a hedge, or you will have a disappointing crop of thin, drawn roots. Shade given by pea or bean plants is ideal. If you are planting radishes in early autumn, select a sunny open site, protected from frosts if possible. Later sowings should have some form of glass protection.

Sowing in the open

Like lettuces, radishes should be sown little and often. Because most varieties are at their best for only a short while after reaching maturity, there is no point in sowing an enormous number of seeds at one time. Successional sowing, every two or three weeks, will give a con-

Harry Smith

1. Well before sowing, dig the soil deeply; add moist peat to very dry or very heavy soils.

2. Work in sifted leafmould or ripe garden compost; avoid digging in heavy manures.

3. Apply a top dressing of bonemeal at the rate of 120 g per sq m (4 oz per sq yd) and fork in lightly.

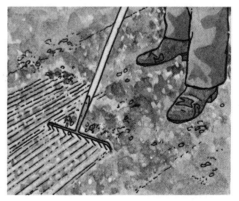

4. Just before sowing, rake the soil surface to a fine tilth and break up any lumps of soil.

5. Make the drills 1.8 cm ($\frac{3}{4}''$) deep, and 10-15 cm (4-6″) apart; be sure they are absolutely level.

6. Sow the seeds thinly, overcrowding leads to foliage rather than root growth.

tinuous, reasonable harvest. An average packet of seeds will be plenty for sowing three 3 m (10′) rows, and should produce over 300 radishes. If you have more seeds than you need, you can share them with friends or store them; under proper conditions, the seeds will retain their vitality for five years.

Radishes are often intercropped with other vegetables—sowing them, for example, on the ridges adjacent to celery trenches. When intercropping in this way, make sure the radishes will not interfere with hoeing and weeding, and there is enough space for access to both crops. Radish seeds are sometimes mixed with slow-germinating seeds, like onion or parsnip. Their distinctive heart-shaped seed leaves mark the rows and the radish roots are soon ready for pulling, leaving space for the long term crops to grow. When you are mixing radish seeds in with another crop, make sure you remove all small slow-growing radishes as soon as the bulk of the radish crop is pulled, to avoid crowding the long term crop.

If you have a very warm, sheltered site, you can sow in the open in early or mid-winter. Do not attempt very early outdoor sowing if the soil is cold, wet and heavy. To improve drainage and to speed growing in winter-sown radishes you can make a slightly raised hot bed in the open. Cover the fermenting material with a 15 cm (6″) layer of fine soil. Some people sow early crops of radishes outdoors in the 10 cm (4″) gap between lines of cloches. The cloches protect the radishes from wind and keep the soil slightly warmer, but you may have difficulty caring for and harvesting the radishes when grown in this way.

Normally outdoor sowings are made from early spring onwards. Sow in drills 1.8 cm ($\frac{3}{4}$″) deep and 10-15 cm (4-6″) apart. Make sure the drills are dead level, so that all the seeds are covered with the same depth of soil.

Radishes must be sown thinly. If you sow them too thickly, you will get a very poor crop; overcrowding leads to foliage rather than root growth. Try to aim for 12-15 seeds per 30 cm (1′) run. Because the seeds are relatively large, you should have little difficulty in sowing them this thinly.

After sowing, rake the soil gently over the radishes to cover them. Never cover the seeds with more than 1.8 cm ($\frac{3}{4}$″) of soil. Then firm down the soil, with the back of a rake or spade. The seeds should germinate from four to ten days after sowing. If thinning is necessary, it should be done as soon as the seedlings are large enough to handle. The smaller salad varieties should be spaced 2.5 cm (1″) apart; the larger salad varieties 3.7-5 cm (1$\frac{1}{2}$-2″) apart.

Radishes for harvesting in winter should be sown in mid to late summer in drills 22 cm (9″) apart, and thinned if necessary so that there is 15 cm (6″) spacing between plants.

A less satisfactory method of sowing radish seeds is sowing them broadcast instead of in drills. Although initially easier and quicker to do, broadcast sowing has several drawbacks. It is much more difficult to control weeds because the radishes are sown over a large and indefinite area; hoeing becomes impossible. Because you cannot control the density of sowing, you will also have more thinning to do. Like other root vegetables radishes do not transplant very well, so the thinnings will be wasted.

Sowing under glass

The earliest radishes of all can be had by growing them on a hot bed in a cold frame in early to mid-winter. For sowing under cold frames select varieties with short leaf growth. Cover the fermenting material with 15 cm (6″) of good soil. Do not mix the soil with the fermenting material as it is the heat and not the rich fertilizer which is essential. Mixing the radish seeds with carrot seeds is an excellent way to make the best use of the frame. The radishes should be ready for pulling in three weeks, and the carrots can grow on. You can sow the radishes in

1. After sowing, tamp down the soil with the head of a rake, so the seeds are in contact with the soil.

2. Thin the seedlings as soon as they are large enough to handle, to 2.5-5cm (1-2″) apart.

3. Dust seedlings with HCH powder as they emerge and again 10 days later, to avoid damage by flea beetle.

4. Protect the seeds and seedlings from birds with small mesh wire netting, bird scarers, or cotton webs.

5. Harvest radishes as soon as they are ready; do not leave them in the ground to get hot and stringy.

6. Large winter radishes can be pulled in autumn and then stored in a box filled with damp sand.

a cold frame in late winter, without a hot bed, but it will take six to eight weeks before they are ready for pulling. Another method of giving glass protection to very early crops is to sow radish seeds in the borders of an unheated greenhouse. Radishes grown under glass should be a minimum of 7.5 cm (3″) apart, with 15 cm (6″) between rows with more space for large types.

Under cloches, radishes can be sown between rows of early lettuce or peas. Grown on their own, five rows of radishes will fit under an average size cloche; with this protection they can be grown outdoors from mid-winter onwards, though cropping may take longer.

Care and development
For early sown crops, under glass and in the open, protection from frost is essential. Cover cloches and frames with newspapers or sacks if a frost is expected. It is best to open the frames during the day to keep the plants well ventilated once they have germinated, shutting the frame at night and covering as necessary. For radishes sown in the open on hot beds, a covering of litter or mats at night helps protect the plants from frost damage. Remove the covering during the day, unless the weather is very cold. A 15 cm (6″) layer of clean straw or branches of evergreen trees or shrubs are also useful for covering the plants in cold conditions.

Moisture is essential; water regularly in warm weather and particularly during the summer. Radish crops will fail if they are checked by lack of water. If you have prepared the ground properly, weeds should not be a problem. Radishes grow very quickly and should be ready to pull before any weeds have time to become established.

Birds like radish seeds and seedlings; if necessary protect them with small mesh wire netting, bird scarers, or webs of black cotton. Birds do not seem to attack radishes past the seedling stage, so the protection need only be temporary.

To avoid damage by flea beetle, dust the seedlings with HCH powder as they appear and again about ten days later.

Although summer radishes do not need additional fertilizers, winter radishes benefit from a dressing of nitro-chalk in early autumn. Apply it at the rate of 30 g per 3 m run (1 oz per 10′ run), to help the radishes make good growth before winter.

Harvesting
Summer radishes are normally harvested three to four weeks after sowing, while they are still young and crisp. If you leave them in the ground until the flowering stems develop, the roots become stringy and have a hot, unpalatable taste. If you have a bumper crop, and more radishes are ready for pulling than your family can sensibly use, harvest them and share them with friends or neighbours. If there is still some surplus, put them straight on the compost heap, as they are rich in nutrients and make good compost. There are some varieties, such as *Cherry Belle* and *Red Prince*, which can remain in the ground for relatively longer periods without splitting or going to seed. The best way to avoid a glut, however, is by frequent and small sowings.

Large winter radishes can either be harvested in autumn and stored in damp sand like carrots, or left in the ground and lifted as needed. They will not become hollow in the centre, as do summer radishes if they are left in the ground for any length of time.

Summer radishes grown on hot beds must be watched very carefully, and picked as soon as they mature, because they are at their best for a few days only.

Exhibition tips
Although four weeks is the average time from sowing to harvesting, it can vary according to weather conditions. Because it is difficult to time the radishes exactly for a particular show date, it is best to make a few small sowings at

1. Sow seed under glass from early winter onwards. Sprinkle the seeds thinly at a depth of 0.5 cm ($\frac{1}{4}$").

2. Open the frame during the day once the seeds have geminated; shut it at night to keep the cold out.

3. If you expect a frost, cover the frame light with sacking or paper to protect the seedlings.

You can also sow radishes in the borders of an unheated greenhouse; make the rows 15 cm (6") apart.

Early radishes can be grown outdoors between rows of cloches used for forcing other crops.

weekly intervals, starting six weeks before the show date.

Do not gather the radishes until just before the show, to avoid wilted foliage. Twenty-four radishes is the usual number shown; they should be as uniform as possible, and all of one variety unless otherwise stated. Select roots of moderate size. The judges will look for fresh, brightly coloured roots with the foliage still attached. Just before the exhibition, wash the radishes under running water until all the soil is removed, and tie the roots in a bundle with green twine. Display with the roots pointing towards the front of the staging.

Black Spanish

China Rose

Varieties

Winter radish
Black Spanish Round: black skin, white flesh; very hardy; lift in winter and store, or leave in the ground and lift as needed. Slice or grate and serve as salad.
China Rose: rose, white-tipped skin, white flesh; oval shaped, 12–15 cm (5–6″) long, 5 cm (2″) in diameter; serve sliced.
Black Spanish Long: black skin, white flesh; similar to Black Spanish Round.
Mino Early: large Japanese variety; roots 37 cm (15″) long, 5 cm (2″) in diameter; mild flavour; useful in autumn and winter.

Spring and summer radish
Cherry Belle: round, smooth, cherry red radish; sweet, mild taste; quick-growing; remains in harvestable condition for a long time.
French Breakfast: red, white-tipped; olive-shaped; crunchy texture; mild and sweet-tasting.
Sparkler: bright red, white-tipped; globe-shaped; very quick-growing.
Inca: bright scarlet; globe-shaped; very firm-textured, even when large.

French Breakfast

Red Forcing

Yellow Gold

Scarlet Globe

Saxerre: round variety, especially suited for early sowings; neat tops; quick to mature.

Half Long: rose red, white-tipped new variety; resistant to pithiness.

Red Prince: new variety; can stand for a long time without going to seed or splitting; grows very large.

Yellow Gold: golden radish, white flesh; egg-shaped; medium flavour.

Red Forcing: early-maturing round variety; useful for cloches, frames, greenhouses.

Scarlet Globe: scarlet roots, pure white flesh; quick-growing.

Red White Tipped: red roots tipped with white; useful for spring and summer sowings; suitable for growing under cloches.

Long White

Long White Icicle: white, tapered shape; 7.5 cm (3″) long; crisp and sweet-tasting; very quick-growing and good for early crops.

Minowase Summer Cross: F$_1$ hybrid; white, tapered shape; 15 cm (6″) long; can be pulled over long period; remains crisp, mild and white without any hot, peppery flavour.

Long White Icicle

Minowase Summer Cross

Pests & Diseases

Radishes are pleasantly trouble-free; because they grow so quickly they are usually harvested well before disease or pests can do much damage. However, like other members of the *Cruciferae* they are subject to infection by several fungal diseases. Provided your garden is clean and weed-free, the radishes are grown as quickly as possible and never allowed to dry out, you are unlikely to encounter much difficulty.

Damping off: this disease is caused by a fungus and infected seedlings will collapse and die at ground level. It is particularly likely to occur if the seedlings are overcrowded or grown in very close, damp conditions. The best preventive measures are to sow seeds thinly and thin them if they are at all overcrowded. Avoid sowing in very wet conditions. Seeds treated with thiram or captan are less vulnerable. If damping off does occur, spray the seedlings with Cheshunt compound.

White blister: if glistening white pustules appear in rings on the leaves of your radishes, they are probably infected with the fungus known as white blister. Although not a serious disease this does disfigure the crop. It is most likely to occur if the radishes are crowded or weak. If white blister does occur, remove and burn all infected leaves. The weed Shepherd's Purse harbours white blister, so make sure your garden is free of this and other cruciferous weeds.

Downy mildew: this is another fungal disease encouraged by poor cultivation. It appears on seedlings and young plants usually on the undersides of the leaves, as white tufts or downy patches. Remove and destroy infected seedlings or leaves. If the plants are badly infected, spray with Bordeaux mixture or zineb.

Club root (finger and toe): this fungal disease usually infects brassicas, but radishes are occasionally damaged. The symptoms are bluish and wilting leaves, and swollen, black, rotting roots which have an unpleasant odour. It is most likely to occur on acid, badly drained soils, so make sure any drainage problems and excessive acidity are corrected before planting. Calomel dust sprinkled in the seed drills before sowing offers some protection. Apply it at the rate of 30 g per 1.5 m (1 oz per 5′) run.

Scab: this fungal disease appears as

Fungal infections appear as woolly growths on the roots or leaves. Radishes grown in wet or overcrowded conditions are most vulnerable.

White downy patches on these radishes are the result of severe infection with downy mildew; it is encouraged by poor cultivation.

Ministry of Agriculture, Fisheries & Food

Ministry of Agriculture, Fisheries & Food

circular, sunken scabby patches on the roots, although occasionally the patches may be raised. The infection is most likely to occur on light, gravelly, hungry soils lacking in organic matter. The most effective preventive measure if your soil is light is to dig in plenty of well-rotted manure, leafmould or vegetable compost well before planting. Avoid overliming your soil, as excessive lime seems to encourage the disease.

Flea beetle: these are the only pests likely to harm radishes. They eat small circular holes in the seedlings and young leaves and will eat older leaves until they are skeletonized and lace-like. They are particularly active in sunny weather from mid to late spring. Adult flea beetles vary in size and colour, but are usually dark blue or black, occasionally with yellow stripes. Because the beetles overwinter in garden debris or rubbish in hedge bottoms, practising good garden hygiene is the best preventative measure. Because they feed on weeds of the *Cruciferae* family, such as Shepherd's Purse and Charlock, make sure your garden is weed-free. Never leave stumps of Brussels sprouts or cabbages in the ground after winter, because flea beetles will feed on them until they can move onto new crops.

If your radishes are healthy and growing quickly, it is unlikely that flea beetles can do severe damage. Water the radishes in dry weather to make sure they are not checked. If the beetles do appear, dust the beds with derris.

GUIDE TO RADISH TROUBLES

Symptoms	Probable causes
Seedlings collapsing at ground level	Damping off
Rings of white pustules on leaves	White blister
White downy patches on undersides of leaves	Downy mildew
Bluish wilting leaves, swollen, foul-smelling roots	Club root
Circular sunken dark scabby patches on roots	Scab
Small circular holes in leaves of seedlings especially	Flea beetle

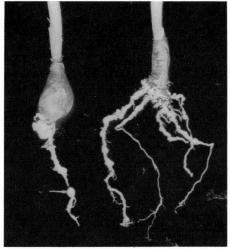

Ministry of Agriculture, Fisheries & Food

These radishes show the main symptom of scab: circular sunken scabby patches on the roots. It is most likely to occur on light soils.

These swollen and distorted roots are infected with club root, a fungal infection associated with badly drained soils.

81

Tomatoes

Lycopersicon esculentum (fam. *Solanaceae*)
Perennial, cultivated as an **annual.**
Sowing to harvesting time: 12-15
weeks, depending on variety.
Size: plants 15 cm-1 m (6″-3′) tall, depending on variety.
Yield: greenhouse tomatoes about 3.6—5.4 kg (8–12 lb) per
plant; outdoor tomatoes 1.8–2.7 kg (4–6 lb).

Tomatoes have always been one of the most popular crops for the amateur gardener. Once regarded almost solely as a greenhouse crop, with the development of new, hardier varieties many people now grow them successfully outdoors. However, it is important to remember that the crop is native to a fairly hot, dry climate. High summer temperatures suit them perfectly, but since that kind of weather cannot be expected every year in a temperate climate, some care must be taken to give tomatoes the right situation.

Tomatoes do not like damp, cool, cloudy conditions, and they cannot stand frosts. Bearing these facts in mind, there is no reason why anyone should not do well with the crop.

Tomatoes cannot be grown outdoors without protection before all danger frost is past. Since frosts can occur right up to the end of spring and may return in early autumn, the time left for cropping is short. Allowing for a growing period of from 12 to 15 weeks, it is possible to sow the seed outdoors in early summer and harvest a crop in late summer, although the farther north one lives the more

hazardous this is. Alternatively you can buy young tomato plants from a nursery. Cloches and frames can be used in several different ways to give you a better chance of a good outdoor crop.

Tomatoes in a cold greenhouse
Most gardeners save growing time by starting tomato plants under glass, even if they are to be transplanted outdoors later. There is no doubt that a greenhouse gives the very best conditions for a successful crop.

Soil
Tomatoes will grow in almost any reasonably rich soil, or even in a basically poor soil if plenty of nutrients are supplied during the season. A greenhouse border soil can be prepared for tomatoes by flooding with water about a month before planting to ensure good water reserves in the subsoil (this is very important) and then, when the soil·is workable, by working in rotted organic matter such as farmyard manure at the rate of one barrowload per 3.5 sq m (per 4 sq yd). About 7-10 days before planting, fork into the top few inches a

1. Sow tomato seeds in a propagator from late winter onward. Space the seeds about 1.5 cm ($\frac{1}{2}$″) apart.

2. When the seedlings are large enough to handle, prick them off into 7.5 cm (3″) pots filled with compost.

3. When the plants are 12.5-15 cm (5-6″) high, transplant them to permanent beds and tie to stakes.

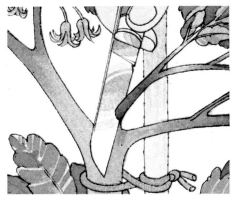

4. If growing single-stem varieties, remove axillary-shoots with a clean knife to control the plant's growth.

5. Give liquid fertilizer as soon as the fruit begins to swell, and repeat every two weeks until harvesting.

6. If growing bush varieties, put dry straw on the ground under the plants to protect them from soil and slugs.

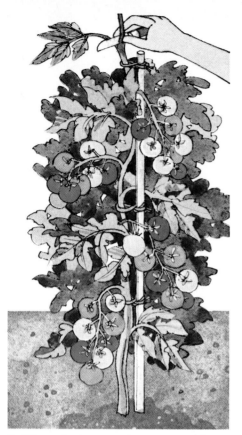

7. When six or seven trusses are ripe, stop the stem one leaf above top truss.

8. Harvest tomatoes as they ripen, leaving the calyx on the fruit.

dressing of a proprietary tomato fertilizer at the rate recommended by the makers. However, after a few years of growing tomatoes in the same soil, pests, bacteria and fungi will multiply in a greenhouse, so precautions must be taken. Either sterilize the soil each year or introduce new compost. A home-made compost can be made of four parts good, sieved loam (preferably a fairly heavy one), one part well-rotted farmyard manure or garden compost, one part coarse sand (all parts by bulk), together with 120 g (4 oz) of a tomato fertilizer, and 22 g ($\frac{3}{4}$ oz) lime per bushel of the mixture. Mix together well, and leave for ten days before use.

Isolate this compost from the soil of the greenhouse floor by growing the plants in boxes or containers separated from the ground by staging or a sheet of polythene.

An increasingly popular method is to use 'grow-bags', which are polythene sacks filled with a suitable compost. Normally bought complete and ready for use from garden supply centres, they prevent the tomato roots coming into contact with contaminated soil.

Sowing

Sow the seed in boxes, pots or trays of well-draining sieved loam or seed compost from mid-winter to early spring. Sow each seed separately, about 0.5 cm ($\frac{1}{4}''$) deep and 2.5 cm ($1''$) apart. Cover the seed-box with glass and brown paper or black polythene until the seeds start to germinate in about 7-14 days. Then remove the covering and

9. Pick by severing the stalk at the knuckle just above the calyx.

10. To ripen green fruit, lay the plants on straw and cover with cloches.

expose the seedlings to as much light as possble, without burning them.

Tomatoes require a germination temperature of about 15°C (60°F). That temperature should be maintained, if possible, throughout the life of the plant; 10°C (50°F) is about the lowest permissable level. 27°C (80°F) is generally considered to be the upper limit. If you are sowing before spring, sow more seed than you might think necessary. This earlier sown seed has a tendency to produce a percentage of inadequate, fern-like plants with ragged leaves— because of poor light. These must be rejected, as they will never crop well.

Transplanting
Transplanting is done in two stages. When the seedlings have grown two seed leaves, and the first true leaf is starting to appear, they need to be moved to give them more growing space. It is usual to transplant them into 7.5 cm (3″) pots, often into peat pots or pots made of black polythene, containing a suitable potting compost for tomatoes. The young plants remain in the pots, in maximum light, to grow into strong, bushy specimens. When they are 12.5-15 cm (5-6″) high they are ready to transplant into their permanent bed, which in the greenhouse can be a pot, box or grow-bag, or a border in the greenhouse floor. At this stage each plant will probably have its first truss of flowers begining to open.

When transplanting, handle carefully, keeping the soil in a ball around the roots. Make sure that both the soil around the plants and the soil into which they are to be set are thoroughly damp, but not saturated. Dig a hole large enough to take the entire contents of the pot in which the plant has been growing. Fill the hole with water if the weather is very dry and quickly transfer the plant and its surrounding compost into it. Press the soil firmly around the stem.

Support
Well-grown tomatoes should yield 3.5-5.5 kg (8-12 lb) of fruit per plant in a season. This is a heavy weight for a plant with a thin stem, so the plant needs support. A string (3 or 4-ply fillis) may be suspended for each plant from an overhead wire, attached at the lower end to a wire hook plunged into the soil, about 23 cm (9″) deep, or to a wire running horizontally about 3.5 cm (1½″) above the soil, along the row of plants. As the plant grows the string is twisted gently round it taking great care not to snap the top of the plant.

Ventilation and shading
Adequate ventilation is essential— stagnant air allows diseases to develop. Open doors and ventilators as much as possible, avoiding draughts to the plants. Attempts to save on heating costs by keeping ventilators closed may result

85

GROWING IN A GREENHOUSE

1. Support plants by twining with fillis string tied to horizontal wires at the top and bottom of the greenhouse. For easy removal later, tie the string to the top wire, as shown in the insert.

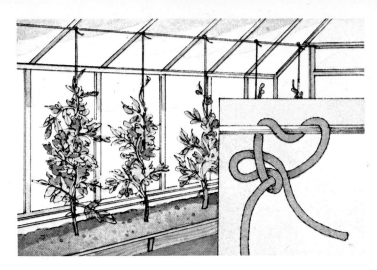

in attacks of moulds and mildews, which thrive in stuffy atmospheres. It is better to keep the plants well aired, albeit slightly chilly.

Provide shade for the plants whenever the temperatures rise above 27°C (80°F), by painting the glass with a proprietary shading compound—there is one which is opaque in sunny weather, and translucent in rain. Alternatively a mixture of quicklime in enough water to make it milk-like, with a little size added for sticking, can be used. You may of course have Venetian or roller blinds attached to the ridge outside the greenhouse which can be used as needed, on the south side. Without shading, leaves will burn and have brown patches.

Pollination

Greenhouse plants may need some assistance with pollination. The pollen needs exactly the right atmospheric humidity to adhere to the female parts of the flowers and to grow down towards the ovule, and sometimes the air in the greenhouse becomes dry. The remedy is to spray the plants and the air with water, preferably in the early morning.

Sideshooting and stopping

As soon as flower trusses start to form, the plant will begin to produce shoots in the joints between stem and leaf. By nature, the tomato is a bushy plant, but allowing these shoots to grow will result in a mass of bushy foliage and a lot of under-sized fruits. Remove sideshoots by pinching them out with thumb and finger as soon as seen. This pinching out should be repeated every two or three days, for the shoots grow quickly. Early morning is the best time for the job.

Towards the end of the season, when the plant is bearing six or seven trusses of fruit, stop the plant, i.e., break off the growing tip cleanly, just above the second leaf above the top truss. The plant can then concentrate all its resources on developing and ripening the fruit on the existing trusses, rather than trying to form more leaves.

De-leafing

Removing the lower leaves of the plant will encourage it to channel its resources into fruit production and improve ventilation close to the soil. But leaves, as long as they are green, are important to a plant—they are food factories—and removal should be approached with caution. Remove only the leaves beneath the lowest truss of fruit and one or two which may be shading it. Using a sharp knife, remove the chosen leaves completely, so that a clean cut is made flush with the stem. Later on in the season, when the life of the plant can be a few

86

2. As fruit sets and swells, remove the leaves below the bottom truss in stages to allow for free air circulation.
3. Spray plants with water each morning to encourage pollination.

4. Keep plants well watered and mulch with peat to conserve moisture. Shade from the hot sun with blinds.
5. To ensure that the fruit swells remove the growing tip at the top wire at least two leaves beyond the last truss.

weeks more at most, remove the leaves more drastically to promote ripening before the cold weather comes.

Any leaves that turn yellow should be removed completely whenever they appear.

Feeding and watering

Tomatoes need plenty of moisture, but not a saturated soil. In borders, they should be watered heavily whenever the soil has become dry on the surface. In containers, daily watering is usually necessary, twice daily in hot weather. In greenhouses, a daily dampening in hot weather is important. This involves spraying the plants, paths, staging and walls of the greenhouse in the morning and at midday.

To produce the highest possible yield tomatoes need generous feeding. Greenhouse tomatoes will certainly benefit from regular application of nutrients. It is quite satisfactory to use a proprietary tomato fertilizer, following the instructions on the container. If you do want to mix your own, 2 parts sulphate of ammonia, 3 of superphosphate and 2 of sulphate of potash (all by weight) make a good, general fertilizer, applied every seven to ten days from the time the fruits begin to swell, at the rate of about a teaspoonful sprinkled in a wide circle round each plant.

Proprietary tomato fertilizers generally contain a fairly high proportion of potash, of which the plant needs liberal supplies for most of its life. Towards the end of the season, however, it will require more nitrogen to support its long stem and foliage. If the top shoot becomes thin and spindly before the plant is at the stage of pinching out, switch to a fertilizer with a higher nitrogen content and lower potash.

If, as the plant grows larger, the lower leaves start to turn yellow between the veins, the plant is probably deficient in magnesium. Correct this by spraying the plants with a solution of magnesium sulphate (Epsom salts) at the rate of 60 g per 4.5 L (2oz per gallon) of water, about once a week. This condition sometimes occurs when a tomato fertilizer with a high potash content has been used too heavily. The plants absorb potash in preference to magnesium.

Harvesting and aftercare

The bottom trusses ripen first. Pick tomatoes before they are quite ripe. Remove the fruit by severing the stalk at the 'knuckle' just above the calyx. Orange-red tomatoes can complete their ripening on a windowsill within a few days, and their removal before they are fully ripe will enable the plant to divert its resources to fruit at an earlier stage of development.

When the first frosts are imminent, harvest all the tomatoes, whatever their colour. Orange, yellow and even some of the green ones will ripen indoors if each is wrapped in paper, and placed in a warm dark place, although they may take several weeks to do so. Those too small to ripen can be used for chutney.

Burn old plants including the roots. Do not put them on the compost heap, for they may well be carrying disease.

Extending the tomato season

The main advantage of taking the trouble and expense of heating a greenhouse in spring to bring on tomato plants is to have tomatoes quite early in the season, in late spring or early summer when prices are still high in the shops. There is not much point in sowing seed in autumn to try for a late winter or early spring crop, because the daylight hours are so short in late autumn and winter that seeds sown before winter will usually lie dormant for many weeks unless artificial lighting is employed, and even then extra lighting will be required for the plants.

It is possible, however, to extend the tomato season until the very end of the year by planting young plants in a greenhouse in mid-summer and providing them with heat when the frosts come.

Ring culture

Ring culture is an excellent method of growing tomatoes. It is best suited to the greenhouse, but may also be used outdoors. With this method, the plants are grown in bottomless 'rings', 23 or 25 cm (9 or 10″) wide and 23 cm (9″) deep, set on a base of moist aggregate (coarse sand, gravel or pebbles). The base may also be made of weathered ash or clinkers, or three parts (by volume) of gravel to one part of vermiculite. The plants develop fibrous roots which draw nourishment from the compost in the rings, and longer roots which derive moisture from the aggregate below it.

The rings should be placed 38 cm (15″) apart in rows 45 cm (18″) apart. Fill each ring to within 1.25 cm ($\frac{1}{2}$″) of the top with potting compost two weeks before planting, in order to give the compost time to warm up. Water compost and aggregate two days before the plants are set out. Give an initial 1 L (2 pts) of water to each plant through the rings, but do not water through the rings again unless the plants wilt in hot weather. Keep the aggregate wet. In about ten days, the roots should reach the aggregate. After this, water the aggregate only, keeping it permanently moist. In a hot summer you will need to give about 2 L ($3\frac{3}{4}$ pt) daily for each plant, but less if the weather is cool and dull.

Make sure plants are properly sup-

Eurocross variety of tomatoes, *thriving in pots against a sunny wall.*

ported, either with stakes put in a week after planting, or with wire and string, as for border plants.

When the fruit begins to form on the first truss, begin giving weekly liquid feeds through the rings at the rate of 1 L (2 pt) per plant. The feed should be high in potash. Halfway through the season, add a 2.5 cm (1″) deep top dressing of fresh potting compost or granulated peat. Otherwise, follow all cultivation and pruning instructions as for greenhouse or outdoor tomatoes.

Outdoor tomatoes

Because the natural home of tomatoes is sunny, choose a plot which gets the maximum amount of sunshine. A site near a wall facing the sun, unshaded by trees, is ideal since the plants also need shelter from wind.

Ideally the soil should be dug over during the autumn and allowed to weather. If it is available, plenty of well-rotted farmyard manure or garden compost should be dug in at the same time, especially if the soil is light.

For outdoor tomatoes the seed is sown in early spring in seed-boxes or other containers in a heated greenhouse. Follow the sowing instructions for greenhouse tomatoes. Transplanted to their outdoor site in early summer, they should produce fruit by late summer and

Grow plants in bottomless rings on a bed of aggregate; feed and water via the rings.

Set bush tomatoes in frames; train forward.

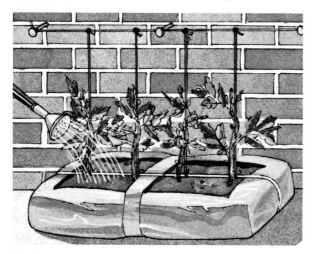

Single-stem plants growing in a peat bag. Support plants with strings tied to a horizontal wire.

Plants grown on stakes in a trench and cloched.

continue cropping until frost checks them. Alternatively, buy young plants for setting out in early summer. After planting in the outdoor bed, cover the plants with flowerpots for several nights, just in case the temperature falls low. When they are growing strongly cover them with a cloche if the temperature falls below 10°C (50°F).

Outdoors, stakes are the simplest method of supporting the plants. Tie the plants to 1.8 m (6′) canes with twine.

Outdoor plants will pollinate themselves without trouble. They will also tolerate temperatures far above 27°C (80°F) if they are given sufficient moisture. If it has been applied, farmyard manure will help to conserve moisture, but during a drought heavy daily watering is necessary, 4-5 litres (a gallon) a day is not too much per plant.

The side-shoots should be pinched out exactly as for greenhouse tomatoes, and the leading shoots should also be stopped after the formation of five trusses or so.

A very rich soil outdoors may provide all the nutrients the tomatoes require, but they are gross feeders, so if the tomato patch is not generously supplied with organic material, liquid feeding exactly as for greenhouse tomatoes will be helpful.

Bush tomatoes

Bush varieties are now available from most seedsmen. They are hardier than ordinary tomatoes and mature more quickly, making them very useful for growing in cooler districts.

The instructions for staking, pinching out side-shoots and stopping leading shoots do not apply to bush tomatoes. Simply allow them to grow freely. They will form small bushes about 45 cm (18″) high and 45 cm (18″) in diameter.

Soil, manuring, watering and general culture are all the same as for ordinary tomatoes. Each plant will produce a mass of fruit, usually much smaller than the ordinary tomato but with a delicious flavour. The stems will sag under the weight of the fruit, so it is advisable to put a layer of straw or plastic over the ground beneath the bushes to keep the fruit clean.

The bush tomatoes include a number of novelties. There are plum-shaped tomatoes, pear-shaped varieties, tomatoes that grow on 'strings' like currants, and yellow bush tomatoes. Some of the smaller varieties may even be grown in pots on window sills or in window boxes.

Growing in a cold frame

Both cold frames and cloches will give a more certain chance of tomatoes developing outdoors. Because the plants can be put out considerably earlier than without protection, the tomatoes thus have a longer period of growth. Choose a slightly shaded, south-facing site, sheltered by a wall if possible, for your frame. Prepare the soil in winter as for outdoor cultivation, and raise the

seedlings in the way described above, or buy young plants. Put the plants in the frame in mid to late spring, or late spring to early summer for bush varieties. Two weeks before planting out, water the soil thoroughly and put the lights on to let the soil warm up. Ten days before transplanting the young plants from their 7.5 cm (3″) pots, give a top dressing of three parts rotted garden compost to one part granulated peat, with 90 g (3 oz) of bonemeal to each bushel of the mixture.

Set the plants towards the back of the frame. Leave 45 cm (18″) each way between single stem (cordon) types and train them along a cane from the back to the front of the frame. Leave the same planting distance between bush varieties. Otherwise, grow as for outdoor tomatoes. Another method of using a frame is to up-end it against a wall and use it to protect three or four tomato plants in pots or boxes.

Growing under cloches

Prepare the soil as for outdoor cultivation. Then, if growing cordon tomatoes, dig a V-shaped trench, 15 cm (6″) deep, 30 cm (12″) wide at the top and 15 cm (6″) wide at the bottom, a week before planting. Add the same top dressing to the bottom of the trench as used for growing under frames.

Set the plants out in mid-spring in warm areas, but a little later in cooler districts. Plant bush types 90 cm (3′) apart and cordon types 45 cm (18″) apart. Extra height can be gained by standing the cloches on bricks, or you could use tall barn cloches for even more height. Remove the cloches from cordon types when the growing tips have nearly reached the tops, and thereafter treat as outdoor tomatoes.

Container growing

Even without a garden, small quantities of tomatoes can be grown in pots, troughs, peat bags or even rings, on patios and balconies. Cultivate the plants in the same way as normal garden tomatoes. All containers except peat bags must hold a minimum depth of 17.5 cm (7″) of a reliable potting compost. Support the plants with canes or by looping a fillis string round the base of each one and tying the other end to a horizontal wire held to a wall with nails. Give regular liquid feeds as well as watering frequently. If using peat bags, water exactly according to manufacturer's instructions.

Exhibition tips

To grow big tomatoes, plants with an unusual number of trusses, or plants with an unusual amount of fruit per truss, try this method: instead of staking the plant, allow it to fall over and grow along the ground. The soil must contain well-rotted manure or garden compost.

Peg the stem down at intervals. At the points where it is pegged it will grow more roots. The plant will then absorb nourishment from perhaps four to eight times as many roots as a normal plant would, and should produce a correspondingly greater weight of fruit. This technique is best employed with indoor tomatoes in a heated greenhouse for an early start, but it can also be successful outdoors.

For a prize-winning truss, select one truss and remove all the others, so that the plant's resources will all be used by the one remaining.

For a single, prize-winning tomato, leave only one on the plant. Spray it frequently with lukewarm water so that it does not burst its skin.

Companion plants

Marigolds, particularly the French variety, help to repel whiteflies, one of the most common of tomato pests, and some commercial growers have marigolds in their tomato greenhouses.

There are also plants which have a detrimental effect on each other. Growing potatoes and tomatoes near each other is to be avoided, because they are members of the same family and therefore attract the same problems.

Pests & Diseases

Tomato moth: the green or pale brown caterpillars of the tomato moth may feed on the leaves and also the fruit, causing great damage. The moths lay their eggs in early to mid-summer, and the caterpillars are seen from mid-summer to early autumn. Caterpillars should be removed by hand and destroyed as soon as they are seen, but if the attack is very bad, spray with fenitrothion.

Eelworm: both the potato root eelworm and the root-knot eelworm can infect tomato roots, causing stunted growth, discoloured leaves and wilting plants. In severe infestations, plants will die. Plants infected by eelworm usually have tiny, cream-coloured cysts on the roots. There is no satisfactory chemical control for eelworm which is available to gardeners. Dig up and burn every scrap of the infected plants, especially the roots, and avoid growing tomatoes on the same ground for at least five years.

Red spider mite: tomatoes grown under glass are especially susceptible to red spider mite. The mites lay their eggs and feed on the undersides of the leaves, producing a reddish mottled look. Fumigation of the greenhouse with azobenzene will help control the pest or spray with derris or malathion.

Whitefly: these can be one of the most troublesome tomato pests, and they can

Serious damage to both fruit and leaves caused by an infestation of white fly.

attack both greenhouse and outdoor plants. The adult flies, which look like tiny moths, lay their eggs on. the undersides of leaves. The immature insects feed on the leaves, secreting honeydew which encourages sooty mould to form. The leaves look greyish and curling. As soon as you see whitefly, spray with resmethrin or malathion.

Leafmould (Cladosporium): this very common greenhouse disease is a fungus which causes yellow patches on the leaves. The undersides of the leaves are often covered in a brown or purple mould. The damage to foliage can be quite severe, and the flowers and fruits can also be affected. Leafmould is most likely to appear where the temperature and humidity at night are high, so maintain good ventilation without drought at such times. Keep an eye open for the disease, which tends to appear from mid-summer, and pick off infected leaves as soon as seen. If necessary, spray with benomyl. Some varieties of tomato are cladosporium-resistant.

Grey mould (Botrytis): this fungus thrives in excessively moist atmospheres such as an unventilated greenhouse. Infected parts (leaves, stems or fruit) grow patches of grey fur, beneath which the plant tissue rots, and eventually the whole plant may die. Prevent by careful ventilation; remove and destroy any infected plants, or parts of plants. The cuts on plants which result from this can be treated with benomyl.

Water or ghost spot: this is caused by the spores of grey mould germinating on the fruits but then drying up because of a change to warm dry conditions. It shows as small, transparent rings on the stem of the fruit and does not cause any real damage. Try not to over-water or splash water on the setting fruit.

Potato blight: this disease also attacks tomatoes, which are members of the same family, so take precautions not to grow potatoes and tomatoes in the same ground or too near to each other. Infected plants have dark brown to black patches on the leaves and eventually develop brown black patches on the fruit. Destroy any affected leaves as soon as you see them. Spraying with Bordeaux mixture in mid to late summer is a good preventative measure.

Verticillium wilt: a fungus disease which infects the roots of the plants, and is soil-borne. First symptoms are the wilting of the top leaves in hot weather, then the lower leaves start to turn yellow; gradually the whole plant wilts and becomes permanently limp. If the stem is cut through horizontally just above soil level, there will be a brown stain in the internal tissues. Infected plants cannot be cured, but mulching close round the stem with moist peat will encourage the plant to put out new

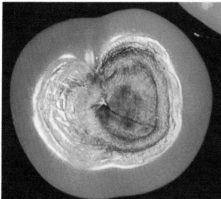

Hard scabs on the fruits produced by severe blossom end rot.

Mottled leaves on a plant suffering from mosaic virus disease.

GUIDE TO TOMATO TROUBLES

Symptom	Probable cause
Irregular holes in leaves, brownish-green caterpillars	Tomato moth
Red mottling on underside of leaves	Red spider mite
Limp, curling leaves, sticky black patches; tiny white flies on undersurface	Whitefly
Small, round leaves; yellow spots, brown fur on underside	Leafmould
Dark brown blotches on leaves, stems and fruit	Potato blight
Mottled yellow and crinkled leaves	Mosaic virus
Bronze brown spots on leaves	Spotted wilt (virus)
Wilting yellow leaves; eventually whole plant wilts	Verticullium wilt
Patches of grey fur	Grey mould
Long, thin, threadlike leaves	Enation mosaic virus
Transparent spots on fruit with 'halo' around them	Water spot
Hard patches on fruit around calyx	Greenback
Yellow patches on red fruit	Blotchy ripening
Hard, sunken dark patch on fruit at blossom end	Blossom end rot
Brown rings around stem at base	Stem rot
Stunted growth; lumps or cysts on roots	Root knot eelworm
	Potato eelworm

healthy roots, which may just save it sufficiently to ripen some of the crop. Spraying the plants daily and lowering the temperature by shading or more ventilation will also help. Destroy infected plants at the end of the season, especially the roots, and sterilize the soil if tomatoes are to be grown there the following season.

Greenback: fruits have hard green patches round the stalk which never colour. The cause may be exposure to too much sun, or lack of potash.

Blotchy ripening: another functional disorder; parts of the fruit remain orange, yellow or pale green and never ripen. Insufficient potash is the cause.

Split fruit: this occurs as a result of irregular water supplies, either because a lot of water has been given after a prolonged dry period in the greenhouse, or because heavy rain follows a drought outdoors.

Stem rot (Didymella): this is a fungus disease which produces a corky infection that girdles the plant stems at soil level. The plants then wilt, and can be completely destroyed. Badly affected plants should be removed and burnt but, if the disease is seen early, spraying with captan may help.

Blossom end rot: this is a condition in which a round, sunken, dark brown or black patch appears on the fruit at the blossom end. It is not caused by a disease but by a severe shortage of water when the fruit is swelling. It can be prevented by regular and adequate watering.

Virus diseases: a good many virus diseases for which there is no cure, can attack tomatoes. Remove any diseased plants immediately. Spotted wilt is the most serious, as it spreads rapidly and can destroy a crop. The young top leaves turn brown, and concentric rings appear on them. The plant stops growing. Thrips spread the disease, especially in the greenhouse, so control these by spraying with malathion, if seen.

Mosaic virus shows as pale green or yellow mottling on the leaves, together with curling and distortion. The fruits will be affected only in severe cases and will show no symptoms.

Yellow mosaic is more serious but rarely seen, with both fruit and leaves mottled with yellow patches. Diseased plants should be dug up and burned.

Enation mosaic is a commonly seen virus trouble, in which the leaves are so badly distorted as to be reduced to long, thin threads, curled and twisted, mainly near the top of the plant. Growth will stop or be slow.

Varieties

Cordon varieties recommended only under glass

Amberly Cross: F₁ hybrid; early and heavy cropper; best for growing under glass; resistant to leafmould and greenback.

Big Boy: F₁ hybrid; enormous tomatoes, each of which can weigh up to 500g (1 lb); excellent flavour. Allow 3 trusses only.

Britain's Breakfast: egg-shaped tomato of excellent flavour; grows best under glass.

Eurocross: F₁ hybrid with several variations; best grown under glass; heavy cropper of large, well-flavoured fruit; resistant to greenback and leafmould.

White: produces yellowish-white tomatoes with a very sweet flavour.

Golden Sunrise: heavy cropper of golden-yellow, medium sized, sweet fruits.

Grower's Pride: vigorous and early F₁ hybrid; reliable indoor variety; excellent cropper; very disease resistant.

Grenadier: new variety; F₁ hybrid; heavy cropper for cold greenhouses; non-greenback; resistant to leafmould.

Britain's Breakfast

Pat Brindley

A-Z Collection

Eurocross

Other cordon varieties, including those for outdoor cultivation

Ailsa Craig: medium-sized fruit of good colour and excellent flavour; early fruiting; can be grown outdoors or under glass.

Alicante: excellent variety which succeeds equally well outdoors or under glass; early fruiting; greenback resistant.

Best of All: large, deep scarlet fruits; heavy cropper; suitable for outdoor growing.

Carters Fruit: grows under glass or outdoors; easy to slice and peel the well-flavoured fruits; very few seeds.

Craigella: form of Ailsa Craig bred for resistance to greenback; reliable cropper of medium-sized, tasty fruits.

Gardener's Delight (Sugar Plum): very popular outdoor variety; long trusses of small but very sweet tomatoes.

Histon Early: one of the earliest of the tall-growing varieties; heavy cropper of bright red, large well-flavoured fruits.

Pixie: very fast ripening; small, compact plants; heavy cropper; hardy, may be grown outdoors.

Sioux: F₁ hybrid; crops early and well; grow outdoors or under glass; medium sized fruits of good quality and taste.

Sub-Arctic Plenty: new type grows very well under most conditions and withstands cold better than most; bite-sized, sweet fruits.

Sunrise: suitable for indoor or outdoor cultivation; medium-sized, well-flavoured fruits.

Sweet 100: new variety; very heavy cropper of tiny, sweet tomatoes; must be staked.

Yellow Perfection

Outdoor Girl

Ailsa Craig

Tiny Tim

Yellow Perfection: suitable for growing outdoors or under glass; heavy cropper; fruits are bright yellow and well flavoured.

Moneymaker: one of the most popular tomatoes; medium-sized, well-shaped scarlet fruits; extremely heavy cropper but rather bland flavour.

MM: F_1 hybrid similar to *Moneymaker;* very early ripening; resistant to leafmould; good all rounder, but especially suitable for cold greenhouses.

Moneycross: another *Moneymaker* type; matures early; resistant to leafmould; fruits of good shape and colour.

Outdoor Girl: one of the best outdoor varieties; very well-flavoured fruits; grows to about 1.2m (4′).

Ronaclave: one of the best tall outdoor varieties; F_1 hybrid; crops early and heavily; large, fleshy fruits; resistant to leafmould, wilt and greenback.

Bush Varieties

The Amateur: one of the earliest and best bush varieties; can be grown indoors or out; heavy cropper of deep red fruits.

Tiny Tim: dwarf bush type suitable for a windowbox; tiny, bright red, almost seedless tomatoes.

Sigmabush: F_1 hybrid; early maturing; high yield; ripens well under poor conditions.

Sleaford Abundance: F_1 hybrid; dwarf bush type; outdoor variety; produces small, bright red tomatoes.